ANTIQUE
COLLECTING

View of Hudgins Gallery, 250 Fort Road, St. Paul,
Minnesota. (Photo: Rodney A. Schwartz)

ANTIQUE
COLLECTING

A Sensible Guide
to Its Art & Mystery

TIMOTHY T. TRENT BLADE

Iowa State University Press / Ames

Timothy Trent Blade is Associate Professor and Curator of Decorative Arts, Department of Design, Housing and Apparel, University of Minnesota, Minneapolis.

© 1989 Iowa State University Press, Ames, Iowa 50010
All rights reserved

Manufactured in the United States of America

First edition, 1989

Library of Congress Cataloging-in-Publication Data

Blade, Timothy T.
    Antique collecting : a sensible guide to its art & mystery / Timothy Trent
Blade.—1st ed.
       p. cm.
    Bibliography: p.
    Includes index.
    ISBN 0-8138-0179-6
    1. Antiques—United States. 2. Antiques—Information services—United
States—Directories.   I. Title.
NK805.B58 1989
745.1'075—dc20
                              89-34130
                                  CIP

For All My Teachers

I have never been able to separate the object from the man, as if the *raison d'être* of each was a function of their mutual existence. But in this relationship, it has always seemed to me, the man is the dupe; of the two it is the object which is the woman. The former believes the latter is the ideal partner who will satisfy his need for love; the latter laughs at her succession of ephemeral lovers for man's life is transcient and that of the objects is eternal. Whenever the latter is abandoned, someone else will soon make himself answerable for its fate. Even if it gets buried it remains alive, merely sleeping while it waits to be unearthed. So the object has the laugh on us all. Time works in its favor, and by taking on the color of its prison walls, it goes unnoticed until the time arrives for newcomers to rediscover its beauties.

Maurice Rheims
The Glorious Obsession

CONTENTS

FOREWORD

Antique collecting has become one of the great passions of a large portion of the American public. To assist them in their pursuits, the shelves of bookstores and libraries are well stocked with lavishly illustrated volumes on varied collectibles, price guides, references on pattern and mark identifications, formulas for furniture refinishing, and dealer directories, all helpful to the collector. Yet few of these works seriously attempt to assist the reader in understanding how the business of antique buying and selling actually is managed.

Professor Timothy Blade has drawn upon his long career as a teacher of decorative arts courses and as a collector to present a broad, balanced, and rational view of the structure of the business of buying and selling antiques. He permits the reader a rare behind-the-scenes look at the trade, uncovering the practices that sometimes make the world of antiques seem a mystery. Dr. Blade focuses on such issues as who the customers are, why they collect, why those called antique dealers encompass such a broad range of types of shops and quality of merchandise, and why the same item may sometimes sell for widely varying prices at different locations. While this book is not about the latest collecting fads, nor is it intended to abet collectors looking for a fast return on their investment, it deals objectively with both these subjects in the larger and more important context of an antique's design quality and condition.

Dealer and customer alike who read this book will gain an increased understanding of the rules and etiquette peculiar to the business. The acquisition and disposition of individual antique items can then be made without the fear that such decisions have been made rashly or in the dark. Dr. Blade's smooth, fluid prose makes this text one which should be required reading before anyone's first foray into the antique marketplace.

John A. Baule, Director
Hennepin County Historical Society
Minneapolis, Minnesota
April 1988

PREFACE

Ever since the first publication in London of Charles Locke Eastlake's revolutionary book, *Hints on Household Taste,* in 1868, with subsequent editions finding considerable acceptance in America, the public of the post-industrial revolution has been continuously warned about the shoddiness of manufactured goods and reminded of the need for constant vigilance to avoid bad taste, bad design, and bad buys. Second only to its usage when referring to used car dealers, the phrase "buyer beware" is most familiar to the antique buyer who is endlessly challenged with being cautious while out in the field. In the case of antiques it is less a matter of the dishonesty of the vendor of the goods that needs to be feared, than it is the trap of trying to make decisions about diverse objects whose condition, authenticity, origin, or intrinsic merit all demand considerable attention. The confusing array of methods whereby antiques are found and purchased is equally demanding. Each phase of this process might well require a lifetime of experience and research to be met with any degree of sensibility.

Buyers of antiquities do not have the recourse of manufacturers' warranties, consumer advocate groups, or government agencies to protect them from poor merchandise or even from slick and deceptive operators in the trade. Their defense is based almost entirely on their own knowledge of the objects, upon reading, experience, and not a little intuition. It is dependent, too, upon a sensitivity to design quality and the ability to judge the relative merits of the endless array of objects competing for one's attention and eventual ownership. Adequate preparation for collectors is also based on their understanding of the antique business itself, its principles, practices, procedures, and its mythology. It is these factors which are the focus of this text.

This book comes as one result of fifteen years of teaching a variety of courses at the University of Minnesota, whose respective subject matters in some way involve the material covered here. The list of courses quite naturally includes the History of Decorative Arts and History of American Furniture. It also entails the philosophy promulgated in Introduction to Design, a class in which students are encouraged, indeed challenged, to increase their visual awareness by evaluating the design quality of the greatest diversity of objects both historic and contemporary, thus expanding their visual literacy. The course whose content most directly relates to this text is Principles of Antique Collecting, offered most recently as an Extension course through the Department of Design, Housing and Apparel, and earlier at several other arts and educational institutions in the Twin Cities. The thematic structure of this course, and the responses of its students over more than a decade, have provided the basis for this writing as well as a vindication of its utility in the marketplace.

The permanent collections of some 8,000 costumes, decorative arts, and textiles of the Department's Goldstein Gallery have provided ample artifacts on which much of the following discussion is based. In the capacity of Curator of Decorative Arts over the last decade, I have identified, assembled, researched, interpreted, and prepared for exhibition thousands of objects connected with topics as diverse as children's toys and clothing, the material culture of death and mourning, sex-role socialization of girls' miniature appliances, collecting decorative arts, tabletop taste, women inventors, and the designer's response to wood. The subsequent dissemination of the information to the public, which resulted from these exhibition activities through programming, publications, and teaching, has provided a forum for the promotion and discussion of much of the theory contained herein.

My participation in innumerable expertise clinics offered as a service to the general public through the programming of the Goldstein Gallery and the Minneapolis Institute of Art has provided additional opportunity for research and observation of what is surely evidence of the grassroots attitude of owners and collectors toward their antiques. In this setting, owners bring cherished heirlooms clutched in their protecting arms, like a pet might be held at the veterinarian, as they anxiously await a diagnosis. Sometimes remarkably wise about their possessions, though more often not, patrons at these affairs typically come armed with the sentiment of family legend and not a little bit of historical misunderstanding about their antiques.

At its most practical level, this book also represents the accumulated information and conclusions drawn from twenty-five years of personal collecting, buying, and selling in a variety of areas, of refinement and redirection of those collections. It is based on an equal number of years of field research in close association with other collectors and dealers in this country and in Europe; I have observed and noted their tactics, trends, tricks, and treachery.

This book is a primer, though, like most primers, its fundamental and straightforward approach should not be confused with simplicity.

Like the classroom courses that generated this material, the text itself should be useful not only to the novice, for whom simplicity and clarity are essential, but also to the more seasoned collector who may have had neither the time nor inclination to consider the process of antique buying in the broader aesthetic, philosophical, or social picture presented here. This is a book about the antique business and the people connected with it more than it is one about the objects they sell. It concerns the why, where, how, and what of collecting antiques, about the personalities in the trade, and the care and use of collections.

ACKNOWLEDGMENTS

During the long period of my own education in the preparation of this material, and in the much shorter time of writing it, I have enjoyed the support of many individuals and institutions. The staff of the Minneapolis Institute of Art, who have regularly invited me to participate in their expertise clinics, and Kathryn Johnson specifically, were instrumental in initiating the course, Principles of Antique Collecting, that I taught and from which this book was generated. Believing a book was in me, my colleague, Prof. Joanne B. Eicher, provided a word processor to hasten my progress. Graduate student Joseph Noonan forced me into the twentieth century by further encouraging my computer literacy. John A. Baule, who has written the generous foreword, provided every conceivable assistance in his capacity as Director of the Hennepin County Historical Society and Museum, and even more as an interested friend.

Innumerable dealers both in this country and in Europe have happily given me information, explanations of the trade, and narratives of their own rich experiences. These especially include Brian Koetser of Phillips, Son & Neale, London; Susanne Fields, Chenil Galleries, London; and American dealers and appraisers Cora Ginzberg of New York, Carroll B. Simmons of Hastings, Minnesota, Thomas H. Murphy of Minneapolis, and Charles M. Hudgins of St. Paul, all of whom recognize a genuine antique long before it bites them. Gary Weibel of G. P. Weibel and Associates provided me with essential inside experience in the estate sale business, its marketing and customer relations. Likewise Jerry Kaufhold taught me the realities of the general-line auction business. The London staffs of the auction houses Christie's; Sotheby's; Phillips, Son & Neale; and Bonham's have been graciously generous in many ways over many years.

Collectors, too, have taught me by their knowledge and love of objects and by the rigorous focuses of their collections. Among them are the late Dr. John Maxon of the Art Institute of Chicago, Profs. Norman and Brenda Canedy and the late Prof. Hylton A. Thomas of the University of Minnesota, Prof. David A. Walsh of the University of

Rochester, N.Y., Prof. David B. Sanford of Macalester College, Harold Sheff, and Rodney Schwartz. One also learns much by bad example from lesser collectors and dealers alike who will all be saved the embarrassment of being mentioned here individually. Particularly important among them in assuring me of the value of a book like this were those who pleaded with me not to reveal their *modi operandi.*

The debt which I owe to my friends and family is of a different kind than that owed to others who are the standard recipients of acknowledgment. To all my faithful friends who have shown interest in this project, and especially Michelle Madson, who has been a constant support in all things, particularly through every stage of this text, I wish to express my warmest gratitude. Finally, I thank my mother, Lois E. O. Blade, who first made me aware, through the splendid furniture made by her grandfather, Samuel William Olson, of the deeper meanings which objects may possess.

ANTIQUE
COLLECTING

1

DEFINITIONS

Antique
Changing Meaning

The term "antique" has had various definitions since its earliest usage. In the Renaissance as early as the late fourteenth century, the rebirth of a new social structure made possible and, indeed, desirable the accumulation of worldly possessions as symbols of newly gained wealth and autonomy, for adorning the surroundings of the wealthy and as an integral part of their quest for beauty and knowledge of their world. In this period the word "antique" made specific reference to the ancient world of Egypt, Greece, and Rome. Thus, objects collected by Renaissance princes and popes from the ancient world were referred to as antique. Today's usage of the term clearly embraces the much larger arena of history that has followed and the objects it has produced.

Age

In 1930 a United States tariff act declared that for an item to be qualified as an antique it had to be made in or before 1830. This was exclusively for the purpose of the protection of American markets from foreign-produced goods of more recent origin. The date of 1830 was, at the time, presumably significant because it also distinguished the approximate advent of machine-made objects caused by the industrial revolution. As the years passed, this law with the arbitrary date of 1830 became more and more restrictive to imported goods.

By 1960 the Revised United States Tariff Act determined that an antique was any item made 100 years prior to its entrance into the country. It is interesting that antique dealers as well as the public seem to support this general age definition of what an antique is. An object that has survived for 100 years seems to have made it over to the side of respectability; it suddenly becomes more significant, more valuable, more desirable, even though it is the same object which once was only fifty years old, or was made last week. Wendell R. Nelson, author of *Houses that Grew* (Amherst, Wis.: Schoolhouse Press, 1985), who has concentrated most of his historical research on the investigation of old

3

houses, confirms the popularity of this viewpoint toward the sacredness of the 100-year qualification among the general public. Owners of old houses, he asserts, irrespective of the actual dates of the buildings, will always claim their house to be 100 years old, seemingly to encourage the attention of historians and the awe of all others. For the readers of this book, and as an aim for collectors, it will become clear that the age of an object per se is of little significance, since the accepted definition

An American milk-glass covered compote, patented June 30, 1874, and dated same year, qualifies as an antique not solely because of its age, but because of its formal design qualities and skill of execution. (Photo: Judy Olausen, courtesy of Goldstein Gallery, University of Minnesota)

of "antique" implies in practice more than merely the year of its manufacture.

George Savage, in *Dictionary of Antiques* (New York: Praeger,
1971), states that an antique is " . . . a work of good quality which is
decorative in intent, made with hand-tools." This short definition is
much more useful than the earlier tariff act description, since it includes
the hand-made quality referred to in that act, but also cites "quality" as

*Many toys are not yet old enough to qualify as antiques
but are extremely desirable as collectibles because of their
quality and the fascination they hold as miniaturizations
of the adult world. American and German miniature toy
appliances, 1900–1940. Goldstein Gallery, gift of Prof.
Holly Schrank, and loan of Gary P. Weibel. (Photo:
Donald Breneman, courtesy of Goldstein Gallery)*

well as decorative intent; yet it does not mention age. This both narrows the parameters of the definition as well as focuses on the most important aspect of an antique, which is the design quality of the object. Savage and others who define "antique" frequently mention the hand-made factor. Some are even more insistent than Savage that nothing which is the product of an impersonal machine can be truly called an antique. This qualification, however, becomes less and less an issue as more and more objects of human production are created through the intervention of the machine. If we were to discount the importance of machine-made objects in the world of antiques, such major collectibles as most Victorian furniture, all manufactured dolls, cast-iron toys, virtually all pressed glass (including Sandwich), all silver plate, and most of what fills up antique shops today, would be ignored. It is hardly reasonable to assume that nothing made after the industrial revolution will ever be "antique" just because it wasn't fabricated by the hands of a single individual whose personality somehow shows through in the object of creation.

In the definition of some objects as antiques, the matter of age is a flexible one, dependent upon the character of the artifact itself. Dolls, for example, are usually considered to be antique if they are 75 years old. The large Antique Automobile Club of the United States considers as "antique" any car made previous to 1930. The Veteran Car Club of Great Britain prefers to call cars made prior to 1917 "veterans," while those produced between 1905 and 1916 are "Edwardian," and those dated up to 1930 are referred to as "vintage." In America, there are also subcategories, and the official recognition of them may vary by state. Special licensing for old cars may include the "collector" category, which covers those vehicles at least twenty years old, but manufactured after 1935, or of a make no longer in production.

Oriental rugs, it is generally agreed, are antique when they are 200 years old. If rugs are newer than that, they are said to be "semi-antique," a term which seems as meaningless and contradictory as being partly pregnant, but nevertheless a standard category of definition in the carpet trade. In Britain, silver must be 100 years old to be antique, at which division the market price virtually doubles. Other sterling, newer than that, is just called "used," and if less than a decade old, is called "new." Regardless of the written definitions which appear in various forms and under diverse auspices, the 100-year qualification seems to be most universally understood and practiced.

While age is often the focus of the categorization of an object as an antique, it is probably in function the least important. No enlightened collector would buy an item solely on the basis of its accumulated years. A collectible is valuable to a potential buyer only if it is useful,

beautiful, curious, historically important, or a financially sound investment. To illustrate this point in my decorative arts courses, I have frequently passed around the class an unglazed clay relic of several inches
in length. Its appearance is unremarkable; it is composed of globs and
bits of fired clay in a cluster. The students invariably examine it with
profound indifference, and most indicate they would not pay a dime for
it at a garage sale. It is neither beautiful, valuable, nor useful. But it is
old. In fact it is 4,000 years old and is a miniature Egyptian burial
substitute for a bunch of grapes found in some anonymous Old
Kingdom grave. The point of this classroom exercise is to demonstrate
that age alone is of no particular merit, and until a meaning is learned
about this object it is difficult to appreciate it solely for its age or its
external qualities alone.

Beauty

Antiques are revered, sought after, and collected for reasons beyond that of their age, and for this reason the other qualities which they
possess must become part of their definition. Beauty is frequently mentioned or implied in defining antique; often the word "decorative" is
used similarly. The twentieth century has not been as fond of this term
as the nineteenth was, because, to modern ears, it implies a preciousness which is unacceptable in today's allegedly practical, sensible, and
bottom-line world. Museum personnel and art historians, of course, use
the phrase "decorative arts" to embrace most of what others would call
"antiques." They do this principally to differentiate Louis XVI furniture,
Sung Dynasty bowls, Georgian silver, Minton vases, and other objects
with some utilitarian intention from those works more traditionally la-
belled as "fine arts," such as paintings, drawings, prints, and sculpture.
Oscar Wilde claimed that all [fine] art was "quite useless," a definition
which suggests that the sole function of art, allegedly, is related to its
beauty or deeper meanings. Clear distinctions between so-called decorative arts and fine arts do not always exist, however, since a Minton or
Tiffany vase may clearly have no utility beyond its beautiful appearance, and many an eighteenth-century print or painting, for example,
was made to be solely decorative.

Some people collect for beauty alone and firmly believe that
there are few contemporary goods which offer the same aesthetic pleasure. This, of course, is an arguable point and one would have to consider the specific object—modern or antique—to test the theory, since
beauty is not the exclusive claim of any one historical period. To insist
that the twentieth century is producing no beautiful, hand-made objects
worthy of collecting (which will eventually accumulate the 100-year

qualification and "become antique") is to ignore the contemporary craft market in America and in Europe. While these craftsmen are not producing the carved and gilded altarpieces, tapestries, or solid silver furniture of the past, they are, nevertheless, remarkably inventive and skilled in their art and are creating quantities of jewelry, furniture, blown glass, ceramics, quilts and other textiles of the highest possible quality. These are the objects that speak most honestly and immediately of our time, and they undoubtedly will become the primary items desired by future collectors because they represent the quality and the uniqueness of our own age.

Collectible

The term "collectible" has crept into the vocabulary of the antique collector in the last several decades because of the diminishing presence of older antiques in an expanding market. Because both collectors and dealers who, because of limited expertise, experience, or money, have been relegated to the activity of buying nonantique goods for their own use or for resale, the category of "collectible" has been established as a convenient term to describe what they own. The attempt on the part of individuals or even professional groups to establish an acceptable definition of this term has not always met with universal agreement. For the purposes of this book, a collectible, simply, is anything which is collected, regardless of age, quality, or significance. Gum wrappers, cigar bands, milk-bottle caps, orange-crate labels, depression glass, Coca-Cola memorabilia, W.P.A. craft projects, Art Deco furniture, or barbed wire may safely be called collectibles. A collectible, essentially, is anything deemed worthy of hoarding which cannot be accurately classified as an antique.

Among certain collectors, there is another category of collectibles that deserves no more than a paragraph to dismiss. Most familiar of these are the immensely popular Christmas plates, Mother's Day plates, certain German figurines of children, plates illustrated with works of the old masters, and privately minted silver and gold commemorative medals, plaques, and ingots. These items are of modern manufacture, and from the onset are self-consciously intended to be collectible. Unlike other legitimate collectibles, they did not enter the market innocently as a genuine production for society's needs such as license plates, restaurant menus, tip trays, or road maps. Collectibles manufactured for their own sake are collected by those who are unimaginative and insecure in their own ability to make value judgments about objects *they* might choose independently, and they are given as gifts to people who are difficult to shop for. Commemorative collectibles, un-

*Some twentieth-century objects have entered the market
self-consciously as ready-made "collectibles" and are
bought by the inexperienced in the uncertain hope that
they will appreciate in value. Danish Christmas spoons
and forks, silver gilt, A. Michelsen Co., Copenhagen,
Denmark, 1932–1970. Goldstein Gallery, gift of Admiral
and Mrs. (Marné Lauritsen) Rowland Haverstick Groff.
(Photo: Judy Olausen, courtesy of Goldstein Gallery)*

like their promotional materials would lead one to believe, are *not*
good investments. So-called "book values" quoted by their manufacturers are largely imaginary—wishful thinking. Collections of plates
from the 1950s through the 1970s are regularly unloaded at auction,
often for prices lower than were paid for them when new. A few early
ones, rare because of truly limited production (not "limited editions" of
100,000) are, indeed, valuable; the rest is little more than ballast on the
ships that bring them to the eager hands of uninformed American collectors.

Collection

> Once an object, no matter how trivial, came
> into his possession, it remained with him for the
> rest of his life.
>
> Albert Goldman, describing
> Elvis Presley in *Elvis*

The distinction between a collection and an accumulation is that a collection has direction. As in prehistoric times, the modern world continues to produce gatherers and hoarders. But, while most of western humankind surrounds itself with the arts of its own hands, or of industry, not everyone has a collection; most merely have accumulations. Accumulations include all the debris of daily living. An accumulation consists of the unconsciously gathered old newspapers, dead television sets, clothes, cars, garden tools, inherited memorabilia, snack sets, tupperware, florist pottery, and empty boxes with which we fill our garages, basements, closets, and attics. An accumulation is the result of the almost imperceptible process of piling one object with another again and again with no regard for its relationship with other objects or with the whole. An accumulation is an admixture.

Collecting in its rightful state is a form of designing; it is selection and organization to produce order and beauty. A collection is a consciously gathered grouping of similar or related objects. When viewed, a collection reveals a common theme or idea which gives its parts relatedness and gives its whole unity. A collection has a focus. The direction that a collection has is influenced by the choice of one or several unifying factors. Antique collectors often define themselves by their collections, and the categories into which their searching falls are almost limitless. Collections can be centered on a historical period, a type or function of object, a material or medium, a handcraft process, the work of a specific artisan, or any number of themes or combinations of themes.

A collection reveals the intelligence and wit of its assembler. The longer one collects, the more likely it is that one will define, redefine, and edit a collection to create further definition, specialization, depth, or breadth as the collector's own knowledge of the subject deepens. They may begin new specialized collections as their knowledge broadens. The saddest kind of collector to observe is the one never willing to admit a mistake and who jealously hoards and cherishes every error along with every treasure. These are the individuals who wantonly purchase whatever amuses them with no regard for the character or quality of the accumulated whole. They are indiscriminate

A true collection is a carefully considered, focussed
selection of objects related by style, function, or theme.
These Danish silver hovedvandsaeg (c. 1780–1850),
which once held perfume, were often betrothal gifts.
Goldstein Gallery, gift of Admiral and Mrs. (Marné
Lauritsen) Rowland Haverstick Groff. (Photo: Judy
Olausen, courtesy of Goldstein Gallery)

Collections may be significant, highly focussed, and specialized without being expensive. Midwestern domestic architecture is the unifying theme of this assemblage of photographic postcards (c. 1890–1915). Gary P. Weibel collection. (Photo: Jim Barbour)

and do not learn from their searching or from the objects they encounter.

As a good collection grows in size, it should also grow in quality and in specificity. For example, a subject as vast as collecting paper goods must have some direction to be significant at all, or even achievable. One might begin by collecting just postcards, then cards depicting scenes from a single state or city. Then, perhaps, only those with architectural views, then exclusively schools, churches, or some further definition. One collector of postcards has attempted since he was a teenager to get a card of every county courthouse in the United States. At age 60 the collector is yet unfinished, though still keenly interested in a task which becomes more difficult and challenging with the addition of each new card.

Narrowing the field by choosing a specialty or two is a natural outcome of one's early collecting, when virtually every object has an equal appeal and anything that looks like a bargain is attractive. The frustration of trying to make sense of the vast array of the available antiques and collectibles soon creates the need to focus one's attention and begin the long process of becoming a specialist. The more knowledgeable collectors become about a subject, the more likely they are to know more than the vendor, and thus the more likely to have the advantage.

Objects without inherent beauty, disconnected from their original use, often have been saved because of their nostalgic value or because of the legends connected with them. Fragment of rope used by Minneapolis school children in 1896 to pull the John H. Stevens House from its original location to Minnehaha Falls; fragment of glass from the face of the Federal Courts Building clock in Minneapolis, built in 1896; glass telephone wire insulator (c. 1900). Hennepin County Historical Society, Minneapolis. (Photo: Jim Barbour)

2

WHY PEOPLE COLLECT

There is only the fight to recover what has been lost
And found and lost again and again: and now, under
    conditions
That seem unpropitious. But perhaps neither gain nor loss.
For us, there is only the trying. The rest is not our business.

                                    T. S. Eliot
                        "East Coker" in *Four Quartets*

Instinct

The instinct of gathering, apparent in insects, birds, and land animals, is also a human activity of prehistoric origins and one which is universal. Gathering of food was undoubtedly at first a survival technique, followed by hoarding, which was a protection and insurance for future survival in times of less abundance. Long after human survival needs were met in the history of humankind, Homo sapiens continued to both gather and hoard. The appearance of man-made objects in earliest times provided yet more things to gather for use and hoarding. The accumulation of food or material objects continues to represent security for those who amass them. Most human beings collect, whether or not they think of themselves as collectors or as having collections.

One cannot separate the gathered objects from the meanings which the assembler gives them. While the gathering of objects was security, it was also power. A tribal chief with more cowry shells, more spears, more cattle, or more wives was given status by those who had less in their charge. The Latin word *pecunia* originally signified property in cattle and continues today to make reference to all property and money. Possession is social and political power. Popes, princes, presidents, and politicians throughout history have created their status by gathering around themselves the various symbols of power such as peasants, voters, tribute money, taxes, gold mines, stock portfolios, coaches, Cadillacs, castles, and condos.

Modern-day suburbanites find the shopping malls a veritable cornucopia of worldly goods to be yearned for, to be hunted down and charged, then to be worn, sat in, eaten off of, driven, or stored for future need. One need not collect antiques to appreciate the strong innate desire to surround one's self with goods and to show them off to neighbors, relatives, and business associates who in turn are stimulated through jealousy, greed, or embarrassment to aspire to ownership of the same.

Children at an early age, even without the intervention of adults, quite instinctively create collections of rocks, shells, insects, and other

The addition of a decorative motif to the masterful shape in clay is an attempt at beauty beyond the requirements of utility, an effort that seems to be an inherent human need. Salt-glazed stoneware crock, W. H. Farrar and Co., Geddes, New York (c. 1850). Goldstein Gallery, gift of Mrs. Karl W. (Ernestine) Elsinger. (Photo: Judy Olausen, courtesy of Goldstein Gallery)

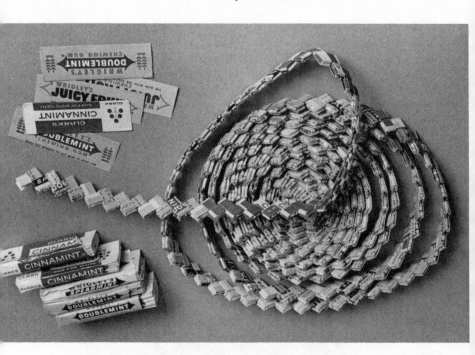

A gum chain testifies to the importance of collecting as an
instinctual childhood activity that involves selection and
organization to create, in this instance, an object of
cultural fad. Gary P. Weibel collection. (Photo: Jim
Barbour)

found objects from their little worlds. In their indomitable curiosity,
they find these objects interesting, beautiful, and intriguing. Their gathering is a normal part of their intellectual development, a way to the
understanding of their world. They have a natural desire to possess
these treasures and, as both child and collection grow, the gathering is
likely to become more self-conscious, more structured; the objects
themselves are more apt to be the products of adult manufacture like
stamps, coins, comic books, baseball cards, and doll clothes. Childhood collecting, so natural at first, might easily be viewed as a kind of
preparation for the more conscious, lifelong process of accumulation
and hoarding so evident in the adult population. The importance which
children attach to their few possessions—blankets, teddy bears, and
nature's bits and pieces—is but a pale reflection of the attitude of most

adults who find solace in an old photograph, a favorite pipe or piece of jewelry, or a comfortable pair of shoes or jeans.

The Hope and the Hunt

> "Why, sometimes I've believed as many as six impossible things before breakfast. . . ."
>
> The Queen, to Alice in Lewis Carroll's
> *Through the Looking Glass and What
> Alice Found There*, Chapter 5

Believing impossible, or nearly impossible, things is not only a necessity for the antique collector, but a matter of serious pursuit for some. Directly related to the instinct of gathering and hoarding, the thrill of the hunt and the undying hope of conquest is a primary motivating factor for anyone seeking antiques. Many collectors consciously choose their favorite method of gathering because they believe it offers them the greatest possibility for discovery. In this pursuit, some will avoid high-quality specialty shops where the value of everything is known by the vendor, and will concentrate their efforts on flea markets, estate sales, and auctions, with the conviction that these settings provide an environment in which "impossible" finds are only just improbable and where undiscovered treasure is thought to sleep in murky corners or sit behind every pile of junk.

The lure of objects has such an overwhelming effect on certain people that any number of collectors find much greater pleasure in finding and buying them than they do in their possession. For them, the act of collecting is what produces the psychological high. Compulsive collectors of this sort fill their houses with things they can never hope to use, enjoy, or even really see very often. The act of searching, discovering, and buying is an act of conquest, power, and a sign of the supremacy of their wits and the weight of their dollars. Even some dealers seem to be seduced by the process itself in accumulating antiques, the resale of which they may view with considerable indifference. Like incurable gamblers, some who buy antiques are almost solely motivated by the hope and conviction that great treasure lies just around the corner and the belief, commonly espoused on T-shirts and bumper stickers, that "He who dies with the most toys wins." For the more balanced collector, if there is such a person, the treasure hunt is still alluring, and it is a process which is unmatched for the anticipation, the tension, the competition, the conquest, and the satisfaction it can bring.

The Meaning of Objects

> For the whole earth is the
> Sepulchre of famous men and
> Their story is not graven
> Only on stone over their
> Native earth but lives on
> Far away without visible
> Symbol woven into the stuff
> Of other men's lives.
>
> Pericles (d. 429 B.C.)

As objects are collected for whatever purpose, they are transformed into associative symbols by the collector. These objects are deliberately or inadvertently imbued with complex meanings sometimes beyond the consciousness even of the owner. The meanings which objects are given by their possessors are often unrelated to the inherent value or utility of the piece. Ordinary photographs, for example, take on extraordinary meaning if the picture is an image of someone we know and love. Handwork wrought by a grandmother or aunt, underwear once owned by Queen Victoria, or a set of false teeth worn by George Washington are accorded deeper importance because of the person who made, used, or cherished them. Repeatedly, auction prices confirm this fact. A spokesman for the Los Angeles auction firm Butterfield and Butterfield, when asked to estimate how much the auction of the estate of flamboyant entertainer Liberace, to be sold in 1988, would bring, declared: "If the property belonged to anyone else, it would bring $2 million to $3 million. But with a collection that is as unique as Liberace's own personality, I would guess between $4 million and $7 million" (*Minneapolis Star and Tribune*, July 1, 1987).

From the Renaissance through the nineteenth century, "curiosity cabinets" were commonplace in every palace and private collection to satisfy the interest for oddities. In the palaces of Germany and Austria in the eighteenth century, *Wunderkämmer* were filled with natural and man-made wonders from the far ends of the earth to enchant aristocratic viewers. No more exaggerated instance of the heightened meanings of objects exists than that of the reliquaries from the Middle Ages — precious gold and silver containers which enshrine purported fragments of the true cross or anatomical parts now separated from their saintly former owners. These objects would have no value if disconnected from their religious significance and ascribed meanings.

History is filled with personalities who collected, and whose collections became an integral part of their own character and a salient feature of their influence over their worlds. Renaissance Pope Julius II collected antiquities from the ancient world, particularly sculpture. Among other works, he bought two ancient sculptures, the Apollo Belvedere and the Laocoön, masterpieces themselves, but equally important for the effect which they had on those artists whom the pope patronized, such as Raphael and Michelangelo, who saw and admired them. Another Renaissance sculptor, Ghiberti, collected intaglio-carved antique gems, miniature sculpture akin to his own large-scale work. In the seventeenth century, Rembrandt eventually bankrupted himself with his passion for collecting the works of other contemporary and earlier painters and sculptors, as well as the elaborate European armour and costumes which he gathered for his own models to wear during sittings. In fact, the public auction of Raphael's portrait of fellow painter Castiglione, in Amsterdam in the 1640s, impressed Rembrandt enough that he made a sketch of it which became the basis of the composition for his own etched self-portrait. In the early eighteenth century, August the Strong, Elector of Saxony, personally assembled the largest collection of Japanese Imari, Chinese blue and white porcelain, and *chine de blanc* figures outside the Orient. The admiration of this magnificent porcelain in Europe became a preoccupation for continental ceramic manufacturers who tried to imitate the material's secret formula. This and other collections of Oriental porcelain had a direct impact upon the designs which emanated from the Meissen factory, an enterprise which August himself owned, patronized, and jealously guarded as a symbol of his power and discriminating taste.

Because objects can be divorced neither from their usage nor from their history, they become the anchors of our memories; they are the things which are remembered; they are the props among which we act out our daily lives. These objects make memorable and, indeed, possible the endless vignettes in which we play our parts. Objects from our childhood, or from someone else's childhood, remind us of an event, a time, a place, an entire ambience, which enhance the meaning and value of the object for the possessor and preserve for history that which was.

The objects of the material culture, of which decorative arts and antiquities are but a small part, are the physical remains which civilization leaves behind as evidence of itself. Lacking other forms of written documentation and recorded history, the ordinary artifacts used in daily life take on extraordinary meaning as they record human aspirations, behavior, and social organization. Objects are never created in a vacuum, and thus within them lies the potential narration of many a tale untold elsewhere. While the so-called "fine arts" may seem remote to many, probably no one but a Tibetan monk can escape the repeated daily contact with the ordinary wares of manufacture. While largely overlooked in their own day, these objects, in time, become the essential mechanisms whereby intimate information about their producers and users may be uncovered by anyone compelled enough to find out from them.

Take a common crockery butter churn, for example. To an archaeologist of the future, such an object would reveal much about the civilization that produced it. The even thickness of its clay walls and the perfection of its cylindrical shape would prove that its maker had access to a wheel. The clay itself and its glaze, and the heat required to fire it, would identify the geological characteristics of its source of origin. The decoration, perhaps nothing more than a graceful number 3 and a well-placed swirl of cobalt blue, might tell of its maker's contact with the English and with the Arabs. The number itself is from the Arabic alphabet, but it also represents the English invention of the gallon as a measurement of liquid volume. The artistic swirl of the number would be evidence of the maker's need for beauty beyond the requirements of utility. The need for the function of the churn attests to the social organization of its producer and user and reveals the agrarian nature of the society. By comparison, the potential revelations of social meanings in a stack of baseball cards or in a Victorian silver cucumber slicer are even more overwhelming.

Personal Enrichment and Education

If, indeed, experience is the best teacher, then the process of searching for and buying antiques is a supremely effective educational process. If the search for order and beauty and truth is a uniquely human characteristic, then it may also be true that that search is as instinctual as the even more fundamental gathering and hoarding process. In the manufacture of hand-made objects, there is often an attempt at perfection or beauty beyond the requirements of utility; this seems to be an inherent human need which knows no geographic bounds. The pursuit of the understanding of antiquities enhances their appreciation. As knowledge about the artifact increases, the perceptions of beauty and meaning are more keenly felt.

No lesson is learned more quickly or more permanently than the one which involves the paying of money for an object whose value has been assessed and determined solely by the buyer. This is particularly true when the action later turns out to have been in error. Regrettably, since antique collectors, like anyone else, are more likely to be introspective after a failure than a success, they may also tend to learn more effectively from their mistakes than from their happier conquests as they analytically determine what went wrong . This education is only slowly and sometimes painfully achieved and what may seem to an observer a "lucky find" or "clear profit" has actually required the investment of considerable time and knowledge gained through experience. In some instances, it is not so much the object itself which is valuable as is the knowledge which helped the finder to recognize it as being valuable.

In the world of antiques, buyers pay for the experience and knowledge of the purveyors when they purchase items from them. This is precisely why prices are generally higher in ascending order at garage sales, flea markets, general-line antique stores, and specialty antique stores, respectively. A price for an identical object purchased at each of these places may be greater as one moves toward specialty because, presumably, the knowledge of the seller regarding the merchandise, as well as the assessment of its monetary worth, increases proportionally. One simply has to know more to run a high-quality antique business.

If knowledge on the part of the seller is power, it is also profit, since the dealer's expertise used in the search for and in the pricing of antiques actually costs the buyer in cold, hard cash. It seems only reasonable then that the buyers who educate themselves have begun to transfer the power, and thus the profit, to themselves.

The process of searching for antiques is a process of increasing one's visual literacy. For the skilled antique buyer, an entire shop or flea market composed of thousands of items is viewed with a considerable ability to visually edit the array of merchandise. This process takes place almost automatically as unwanted items are visually discarded and sought-for items are focussed on. This is a process which is so second nature to the seasoned collector that it is only consciously recognized by them when they are accompanied on such field trips by a novice for whom every item in a shop is equally commanding of attention. In an entire auditorium filled with a million objects flowing out of the booths of several hundred dealers, an experienced shopper can zero in on all the hatpin holders, mourning jewelry, or cameo glass the place has to offer.

The more one sees, the more knowledge is gained by the perceptive observer who assimilates the information. In this process inevitable comparisons take place, nuances of difference in similar objects become apparent. Levels of quality and perfection of design and condition are noticeable as information is stored and shuffled in the collector's head. It is ultimately on the basis of comparison that all judgments are made and those judgments are most rational when the experience on which they are based is broad.

The vast number of publications on antiques are rich sources of information for the collector for the identification of antiques, the determination of trends, pricing, and markets for buying and selling. (Photo: Jim Barbour)

Nostalgia

Wendell Garrett, the distinguished editor of the magazine *Antiques,* said of collecting that some people are motivated by nostalgia. "The fad for folk art is what I call homesickness for a happy childhood. Life is so complicated today that people look backward instead of forward." The urge to indulge sentiment by attempting to recapture the past prompts others to surround themselves with objects which are

Regular visits to museums and exhibitions prepare wise collectors for the antique market by giving them criteria of quality against which they may compare objects they wish to purchase. View of Bean Gallery of Decorative Arts, Minneapolis Institute of Art. (Courtesy of Minneapolis Institute of Art)

reminiscent (only to those who did not have to suffer its trials and indignities) of simpler times. One of the most visible public figures who collected, Nelson Rockefeller, once stated his own philosophy of collecting: "I think there is so much tension and pressure in the world . . . that one gets tired and short-tempered, and if you can come back at the end of the day to an environment of beauty, that has a very important effect on one's sense of tranquility and sense of peace."

Investment

Historically, great collectors, bankers, businessmen, industrialists, and even governments have perceived art and antiquities as valuable assets, to be bought when possession and price seemed right, kept as they appreciated, and sold in hard times, or to generate cash for new purchases. The possession of art and antiques, considered by many to be frivolous, is nevertheless viewed, even in times of national or world economic crisis, as more dependable and stable than stocks, bonds, or even currencies. The uninterrupted and sometimes even intensified activity of antique and art trading in this country and in Europe during periods of financial crises and in wartime is sufficient evidence to indicate the physical security value of such property.

Despite this phenomenon, collecting specifically for investment can be the single most dangerous motivation for buying antiques for any collector, and for the novice it is sheer folly. Yet, because antiques have the deserved reputation of being inherently valuable, and because they are known to appreciate with time and favor, hopeful buyers continue to purchase old things with the expectation that they will become more valuable with age and that they might sell them at a profit. The established fact that good antiques may also be good investments, however, does not necessarily mean that they provide ready cash for the collector's pocket. Antiques *are* valuable for their inherent beauty and condition. Antiques *become* valuable assets because they appreciate through the action of certain external factors. For one, they become rarer as others of their kind are lost with the passage of time. In other cases they gain significance because of their connections with historic events or persons. In still other instances their demand or popularity in the marketplace increases through their discovery, and with the increase in knowledge about them. The appreciating nature of antiques, while one important consideration for the average collector, is best thought of as a happy by-product of wise antique buying and not as an end in itself.

For many collectors, the concept of investment is really a moot point, since the proof of antiques' monetary worth necessitates the *sale* of the precious objects which they have so jealously gathered to themselves. Theoretically, at least, no antique is worth anything as an investment unless its owner is willing to sell it at some point. Many collectors practically impoverish themselves with their passion for antiques, spending every spare bit of cash on more acquisitions. These people whose motivation for buying is the love of the objects, are unlikely to sell them at all, even if the mortgage payment is due. In any event, by accumulating antiquities in quantity, compulsive collectors are much more likely to go bankrupt than they are to enrich their personal fortunes.

In the instances where a collector does want to sell, it should be remembered that any kind of successful investment, antique or otherwise, requires the purchase of objects or commodities at a *wholesale* price, and the selling of them at *retail*. This is far easier for a dealer to do within the setting of an antique shop than it is for the private collector. For one thing the collector does not have access to the broad audience of buyers that the dealer does. For another, a dealer may have an item on the floor for a year before it sells, while the collector trying to sell privately may not be as patient, a fault which sometimes causes him or her to sell for less than the item is really worth. To realize top dollar, a collector would have to sell directly to another collector, rather than to a dealer who would pay only 50% of its market value or to an auctioneer who would charge 25% or more to sell it.

It is wise for collectors who imagine that great profit may be theirs through the buying and selling of antiques to consider the activity of those who spend their lives doing so—the dealers in antiques and collectibles. It seems only reasonable that if anyone is going to make a profit on antiques, it will be the dealers who, after all, should be the most knowledgeable about old objects. They are probably also the most alert to plentiful and cheap sources, current prices and trends, and the best retail outlets. Dealers who handle thousands of objects yearly are, presumably, also more cautious of shoddy goods, shady dealers, and clever fakes.

Despite the advantages of skill which they may possess, of the tens of thousands of dealers in this country, few are rich, and most are the owners of ordinary small businesses who struggle to pay the overhead and manage to keep a few dollars for themselves. Contrary to popular opinion, dealers can seldom even afford to keep the "good stuff" for themselves; they need to sell it quickly and put part of the profit back into more inventory. In this financially precarious setting, it is not surprising that a very large number of dealers are the husbands or wives of spouses who work at something else for a regular paycheck. Many other dealers are part-time operators who can afford to do it only as a second source of income, or as an amusing and occasionally profitable hobby.

Anyone who has an interest in antiques as investment soon realizes that not all antiques appreciate at the same rate, some appreciate very little, and some, because they fall from public favor, actually depreciate if one considers only their current market value. Great paintings, documented period furniture, early silver, and other objects of high quality and distinction, which are generally beyond the reach of ordinary collectors, will naturally appreciate the fastest because there are fewer of them in the market in relation to their demand. On the other hand, buying up scads of depression glass, or "flow blue" or silver plate, even at reasonable prices, is unlikely to make the seller of the same more than a modest profit.

Often those who consider investing in antiques forget the crucial factor which time plays in the effort. Sometimes the appreciation (monetary or public) which some antiques enjoy takes many years. Having money which is not gaining interest tied up for very long in speculative goods is best left to those few who are intensely sensitive to the market and its trends over the long haul. Another obvious danger to anyone setting out exclusively to make money on antiques as investment is that they are obliged too often to buy and possess objects which they do not personally like and which give them no pleasure.

The question of who then *does* make money on antiques is best answered by stating that many people make *some* profit on antiques, and a very few make a lot more. As with any business venture, the profit derived from antiques is closely correlated with the amount of capital invested. Dealers who have tens or even hundreds of thousands of dollars to buy inventory at a good price are naturally the most likely to turn a handsome profit. An eighteenth-century Boston serpentine chest of drawers bought for $16,000 might be sold a month later for $21,500. The margin of markup can reasonably be less than the usual 100% when figures of this kind are involved. The low-end dealer, however, who may spend just as much time as the furniture dealer (though far less money) finding two boxes of miscellaneous glassware to resell will have to realize a 100% profit from them to meet expenses. In the "mom and pop" antique shops whose stock regularly looks like no more than $100 was spent for any item, one expects low gross receipts because of the typically small initial investment. It is often, unfortunately, a cycle whose mediocrity is self-perpetuating.

At one end of the odd continuum of humanity known as collectors are the purists and aesthetes who collect for the beauty and lure of the objects themselves. For these people, the crass concept of antiques as investment is nearly unthinkable. Having once gathered antiquities to their bosoms, they only seek to preserve them, admire them, and eventually bequeath them to their heirs. At the other extreme are collectors who are indifferent to the charm of what they handle and objectively view antiques only as potentially profitable merchandise. Most collectors fall somewhere in between. Even those who collect for the love of the object, the fascination for history, or the thrill of the hunt will eventually refine or redirect their collections and quite naturally will need to sell unwanted items. Any collector who has grown tired of an antique and has tried to sell it is keenly aware how tiresome and humbling an experience it is to find someone willing to pay even what was paid for it in the first place. Since most collections consist of objects bought at retail, the selling of them, even years later, may not bring much profit. Even a modest profit here and there will convince the seller that buying antiques specifically for investment is hard work at best, and in some cases may lead to disappointment or disaster.

3

WHO COLLECTS

> They were all there like vultures on the bedpost.
> Two dealers from the city, dressed like they'd just
> come from the funeral, were holding numbers
> one and two. Behind them a handful of local
> collectors in overstretched polyester waited in
> line with boxes to hold the prettys they would
> take by the armful off the mantle and the dining
> room table. The people next door were there
> too, not for the antiques, but curious to see the
> inside of the house their dead neighbor had
> never invited them in to see in thirty years.
>
> Sinclair Stevenson
> *The Only Game in Town*

The mere mention of the word "antique" usually conjures up an image of a little old lady in a Victorian parlor draped with brocade and lace, filled with carved furniture and shelves spilling over with knick-knacks. The other most often-held image of a collector is of someone who is rich. However, attending any large antique show is sufficient evidence that all kinds of people collect all kinds of antiques. The populace gathered for such an event is indistinguishable from those attending a house and garden show, a sports and camping show, or a Billy Graham rally. Here one might see little old ladies buying cut glass; middle-aged persons finding delicate, painted porcelain or dolls; teenagers adding baseball cards or beer cans to their collections; big men wearing white shoes and matching belts, searching endlessly for railroad memorabilia or guns; young couples buying cute primitives to furnish their cozy bungalows; and ascetic youths with glasses looking frantically through stacks of postcards for any which might have streetcars on them. This varied view of collectors, while not a scientific sampling, is one seen anywhere throughout the land where antiques or collectibles are to be found.

In 1976, Charles E. Treas, professor of marketing in the School of Business at the University of Mississippi, and Dalton E. Brannen, graduate student, devised a questionnaire and surveyed the readership of

American Collector to determine exactly who is collecting. Through this limited survey, one of the few on the topic, some interesting, though perhaps not surprising, conclusions were drawn. Nearly everyone who collects is either employed (81%)—therefore likely under 65— or retired (18%). The average household of the collector was slightly smaller than the U.S. average. The median income of the collector was slightly over the national median. Most collectors surveyed were high school graduates and 37% held college degrees—three times the national average. The largest sample of collectors were white-collar workers (71%), followed by blue-collar workers (18%) and farmers (3%). Twenty-two percent were also dealers. The least surprising result of the survey was that 98% reported that they were actively collecting at the present time. Inactive collectors, apparently, are as rare as retired dealers.

In the same year that the *American Collector* survey was compiled, a similar survey of the readership of *American Antiques* was published in the latter. The results were similar to the findings of the *American Collector* that most collectors earn above the average annual income (75%). This survey also showed that the collectors they interviewed were free to indulge their interests because 61% were either single (19%) or were married but not raising a family (42%). The average amount spent on a total collection was reported to be over $3,200 versus the figure of $4,000 found in the *Collector* survey. Also, a poll of the specific collecting interests of readers revealed that furniture, glass, pewter, clocks, and porcelain, in that order, were the favorites.

4

WHERE TO COLLECT

The buying and selling of antiques can be done at almost any level. The degree of commitment, the amount of monetary investment, or the requisite of expertise to start a business may vary considerably depending on the setting where one chooses to sell one's goods. Descriptions and explanations of the following settings can help collectors in determining where it is worth spending their time and money, and on what.

Antique Shops and Their Types

> Choice antiques bought, choice antiques sold
> Choice antiques in the shop, nine days old!
> Father likes 'em bright, Mother black with mold,
> But I like 'em in the shop, nine days old!
>
> Alice van Leer Carrick
> and Kenneth Allen Robinson
> "Mother Goose for Antique Collectors"
> (Reprinted from *The Saturday Evening Post*,
> © 1927 by The Curtis Publishing Co.)

For the amateur collector as well as the general public, the antique store is the most visible presence of the trade. Antique shops are more plentiful and accessible than any other setting in which antiques are bought and sold. They are far more obvious to most people than auction houses or any of the less permanent forms of vending collectibles such as estate sales and flea markets. These shops line many avenues of large cities and suburbs and dot the rural countryside. There are about 30,000 antique shops in the United States, give or take the few thousand that are regularly going into or out of business.

The general business economy of the antique retail trade is at some variance with that of most other vendors of goods. The most dramatic differences are those of competition and the supply of goods. The competition among dealers for interested buyers is almost nonexistent; this is not so with other businesses. It would be unthinkable, for instance, that twenty bakeries or hardware stores or even gas stations could all make a profit if grouped within a few thousand yards of one another. Yet antique stores not only survive under this arrangement but seem to thrive. The only other retail trade which comes to mind in which this system seems to work is that of fast-food restaurants which populate the commercial strips of our cities. The reasons for the survival of each is simple; they all have something different to sell.

The competition which does exist in the antique trade is fierce, but it comes not in the selling of goods but in the buying of them. No antique store really ever went out of business because it couldn't find customers. They generally fail because they cannot keep up a steady flow of quality merchandise to fill their shops. Many an enthusiastic and hopeful beginner in the business has discovered, like most collectors, that good antiques are hard to find, and even harder to find at wholesale prices. Even obscurely situated shops will attract clients if their stock is consistently good and fairly priced. Unlike most retail businesses that order new merchandise from wholesalers, catalogs, or from salesmen regularly approaching their showrooms, the antique dealer has no such sources. When shortages of new goods are discovered, more can be manufactured. Clearly this is not the case with antiques—at least not usually.

The supply of antiques in our society remains relatively constant; some are destroyed by time, use, and peril, and others are slowly added to the market by virtue of their advancing age and high quality. The number of potential customers for these goods, however, seems to be increasing. A general increase in "disposable income" through the increasing occurrence of the two-salary family is but one factor in the growth of the popularity of antiques along with all other consumer goods. Other factors certainly include the increased awareness of antiques as attractive and prudent alternatives to the purchase of new goods. This is encouraged by the popular press, by community education classes, and by everything from home decorating magazines to the dramatic increase in the number and quality of publications written on the specialized aspects of collecting that have appeared in the past twenty years. Antique dealers, in order to stock their shops, must compete in the purchase of antiques not only with other dealers who must pay wholesale prices for what they find, but with private collectors who are willing to pay retail.

The public perception of an antique dealer, particularly one who keeps a shop, is of one who is shrewd, deceptive, and opportunistic to the point of being dishonest. For all the disparaging remarks and disagreeable characteristics which have been attributed to antique dealers, there are undoubtedly some who deserve such labelling. The dealer who owns an antique shop and intends to enjoy a long and healthy business, however, has only two commodities to sell: quality goods and a reputation for honesty. In many ways, the keeper of an antique shop is even more vulnerable to the liabilities of a bad name than other retailers, since their customers for antiques, already limited in number by the nature of what they buy, deal much more directly with the proprietor than in many other kinds of retail businesses and thus depend upon personal integrity all the more.

Like any other retail establishment, antique shops run the entire gamut from the most intimidating fortresses of respectability to the thoroughly loathsome pits of junk. Curiously, there is a place for each of them under the sun; usually, the merchandise distributed among them seeks its own level. And so do the customers. To adequately characterize the experience of buying antiques in the setting of a shop, it is necessary to differentiate their types.

The Upper Crust

The highest level of antique shops, generally speaking, is found often, though not always, in larger metropolitan areas and in the biggest cities of the country. Primary among them are the Fifth Avenue, Madison Avenue, and West 57th Street shops in New York City. These and others in Massachusetts, Connecticut, Delaware, and Pennsylvania are the preeminent dealers in fine American and English antiquities and in many ways provide the benchmark against which all other lesser enterprises are judged. They certainly represent the level to which many humbler dealers aspire. These are the dealers who regularly are called upon to supply the White House, the Department of State, and the nation's great historic restorations with furniture and accessories of supreme quality. Traditionally these firms have endured for several generations. Invariably the name of the shop is that of the family name, a symbol of their continuity, integrity, and personal service.

The stock displayed in these shops is of museum quality, and their management often rejects for purchase a piece of furniture which has been altered, even minimally, refinished, or has replaced hardware. Their full-page, well-placed, color advertisements in the most respected monthly antique periodicals reveal their success and their distinguished standards. Shops of the quality of Israel Sack, David Stockwell, Bernard and S. Dean Levy, or John Walton are frequently in a position to provide complete provenance of ownership of an antique and even occasionally cite a scholarly publication which has included the piece they feature. They may even mention that they have had the honor to offer this object to the public two or three times in as many decades. This

High-quality antique shops offer merchandise that is both
earlier and rarer than mere collectibles. Their contents are
often most attractive to the sophisticated collector who
knows their true value. View of Hudgins Gallery, 250 Fort
Road, St. Paul, Minnesota. (Photo: Rodney A. Schwartz)

both confirms family trust and the solid, appreciating nature of their
goods.

In the rarified and invigorating atmosphere of these shops the
customer is not met with the smell of fresh varnish or by a dealer in
work clothes eating his or her lunch. Formal business wear and hushed
tones are the general rule here for both seller and buyer. These dealers,
like most others at any level, know who their customers are. They can
size up anyone who enters the shop by the way they dress and speak
and after a minute of conversation they usually know whether or not
the patron is seriously interested in buying, or indeed is in a position to
buy such expensive merchandise. These dealers have the most sophisticated business acumen, and are as knowledgeable about the fluctua-

tions of the stock market as it affects their business as they are about the authenticity and correctness of their merchandise. This expertise is essential when dealing with single items whose value is in the tens—or hundreds—of thousands of dollars.

For many of these upper-echelon dealers, the search for antiques to compose the stock of their trade is one which involves a balanced combination of intelligence, sophistication, subtlety, and grace, as well as a capacity for persuasive argument and a banker's objectivity about the deal. The items they desire are often in the hands of families who have owned them for generations, and who must be persuaded to let them go by a guarantee of a very high price tag. They must be aware at all times of who owns what, of marriages, divorces, sickness, death, and any other change of family structure which might cause antiques of this level to be sold. They must be in the right place at the right time. Unlike dealers working at a lower level, they are seldom negotiating with people who do not know what they have, though, perhaps, in an earlier day they were. Often they know the entire history of the ownership of the piece before they make their offer.

In both America and Europe, these shops present a severe facade to the public. They often display but a single piece of furniture in the window, and richly framed paintings are supported on solitary pedestals sparsely placed around the galleries. Despite the excellence of these shops and the often-intimidating quality of the goods they offer, the proprietors, once assured of the customer's interest and good intentions, are usually approachable and helpful. Most of these antiquarians keep a very low-key demeanor, and seem almost indifferent to the selling of their goods. Serious customers come to them, they don't have to go looking for buyers; fine quality antiques have a way of selling themselves. Many of these dealers will seek out among their contacts supreme pieces for their clients; they are often asked to be anonymous agents in the purchase of items at public auction for customers who wish to remain unidentified. There are few greater assets for a dealer than the names and telephone numbers of ready customers for certain kinds of goods. Patrons of these shops are those who are rich, knowledgeable (or who have the good advice of others), and who are confident in their demand for the best quality, secure in the knowledge that it is also a sound financial investment.

These are the dealers who write books about the trade, about whom books are written, and who act as advisors and authenticators to others. The highest-level shops, however, are not what the average collector haunts. The beginning collector, and even the more sophisticated ones of modest means, may never enter the hallowed galleries of such establishments. But it is well for any collector to know of their existence, and even politely visit their premises. For what these upper-crust shops do, if the "trickle-down" economic theory has any validity, at least indirectly affects the commerce of the lowliest shop. High prices achieved at the best establishments for certain kinds of merchandise affect both the price of related if lesser goods, and even the popularity of such goods.

Doorbell Dealers

More plentiful, and sometimes more accessible for many collectors of antiques, are the shops which are fancy, expensive, and in good neighborhoods. Because of the proprietors' lesser qualifications and more limited budgets or family fortunes, they may not be dealing exclusively with objects whose credentials are impeccable or whose designs are universally admired. Certainly they are not dealing with objects whose value in the marketplace is unarguable or pace setting. These shops can be identified easily by the richness of surfaces which they present to the public, for the prisms, cut glass, export wares, pretty European hand-painted porcelain, showy Oriental furniture, bronzes, brocades, tapestries, and plenty of "French" things.

The proprietors of these shops are either men or women, single or paired, sometimes in odd combinations, whose personal appearances and affectations are usually commensurate with those of the interiors they guard. They wear lots of jewelry and have their eyeglasses on a chain; they often have dogs or cats. More often than not, these owners have an unrealistic notion of what their things are actually worth and an inflated view of their own expertise. Their shops always have a doorbell which must be rung (and responded to) in order that ingress may be accomplished. A memorable shop of this type in Chicago posted a neatly lettered sign on its door which read, "If you are an intelligent, knowledgeable and articulate person who is seriously interested in what we sell, please ring the bell. If not, STAY AWAY." The shop is no longer in business for obvious reasons, as only the heartiest souls, confident of their own impeccable credentials, ever dared enter to bother the proprietor.

Once inside a doorbell shop, the customer is often made to feel uncomfortable by the sheer visual density of the displays, the unrelenting abundance of ornamentation, and, somehow, the sameness of the merchandise. Purchasing stock for a shop of this kind apparently is done with the notion that, indeed, more is more. The beauty which simplicity or understatement may have to offer has usually escaped the buyers for such places. Rarely do shops of this kind ever bring forth bargains for the collector because at any level of collecting, wholesale or retail, fancy goods almost always bring fancy prices and the "sleepers" among them are very few. Even amateurs unloading richly decorative objects imagine them to be especially valuable and charge accordingly.

Despite their pretentious character, these shops do have their advantages. For one thing, the condition of the merchandise is consistently good and the quality of its manufacture, if not always of its design, is predictably high. The specialized collector who is looking for a particular grand or rare object, and is willing to pay top dollar for it, may do well to search out such shops. For another, one never has to wallow through boxes of miscellaneous trash and second-rate collectibles. The selection of every object on the premises has been done carefully in advance by a very particular, and sometimes even knowledgeable, dealer who, quite rightly, is charging the customer for the editing process. The items are clean, polished, and complete. There is no furniture-in-the-rough, no farm tools or rusty lanterns, and probably no partial sets of glassware or china. These are often the dealers who pay the highest prices for antiques at auction and, thus, must charge the most to the customer. The specialty of these shops is that of a consistent viewpoint toward the complex character and design of the varied stock, rather than a limited specialty subject category or historic time period.

Specialty Shops

Antique dealers who have entire shops filled exclusively with Tiffany lamps, art pottery, Federal furniture, Orientalia, eighteenth-century silver, Barbizon paintings, scrubbed pine primitives, folk art, Shaker crafts, Oriental rugs, or Russian antiquities may safely be described as being specialty shops. In larger cities where specialized collectors are more plentiful, the specialty antique shop is more likely to thrive. They are more apt to be run by dealers who have a personal interest in their merchandise, and whose own individual tastes run parallel to what they sell to others. These proprietors are usually people who, by virtue of their own collecting, have become specialists and thus, to some degree, experts in their field. Like the doorbell dealers, these specialists provide a service to the customer who has neither the time nor inclination to grope through endless miscellany to find something of quality in their area of interest. These shops cater to more advanced collectors who know precisely what they want and are willing to pay for the privilege of being unmolested by the sight of goods which are of peripheral interest. Many collectors do not appreciate this setting; for them the pleasure, tension, and mystery of the search as well as the hope of discovering the undiscovered is all but eliminated.

By Appointment Only

An accurate count of the number of dealers who do business from their own homes by appointment only is difficult to ascertain. Certainly there must be thousands throughout the country. These low-profile operators usually are not visible to the general antique-buying public. They may or may not do any regular advertising, and most do not have signs to designate the location of their establishments. Those who do advertise may do so in the Yellow Pages or in national periodicals, and sometimes are better known nationally than they are in their own communities. Most seasoned collectors know of these dealers and visit them regularly. Word-of-mouth is their best publicity, and they often do a majority of their business with a regular clientele established over many years of practice. Not infrequently they act as "finders" of antiques for their long-time customers. They may devote full time to the buying and selling of antiques, or they may work at it only evenings and weekends in addition to their regular job.

Because by-appointment-only dealers operate out of the limited space of a basement, garage, or spare room, the merchandise which they offer for sale may be more limited in amount, and often is more specialized in its direction. Occasionally, though, these dealers will have a general-line inventory. Their pricing of goods tends to be lower than shop prices because of a lower overhead. Appointment dealers have more personal relationships with their customers, know most of them by name, and are likely to be quite familiar with the collections and tastes of each one. They often call clients when they receive a piece which may interest them, and some use mailing lists to inform customers of new acquisitions. Not unlike the "pickers," to be considered later, the appointment dealer is concerned with rapid turnover of antiques, because there is little room to store them. Thus, price negotiations in this setting are a perfectly reasonable expectation. For the customer, it is wise to make regular visits or calls to these dealers to keep abreast of new merchandise.

General-line Shops

The most numerous antique shops in this country, and in many ways the most fun to shop in, are those which offer an unpredictable assortment of merchandise with as much variety to be found in the type, age, and quality of the goods as in the pricing of them. These shops are typical of small businesses everywhere. The percentage and quality of the inventory offered at the upper level is limited by the bankroll or credit line available, as well as by the degree of knowledge and daring of the small operator. Modest profits are generally directed back into the business to purchase more stock which will be similar to what has been sold. Even more so than antique dealers mentioned earlier, general-line dealers particularly depend on buying cheaply, often in box lots, and from sources less knowledgeable than themselves.

Unless backed by a huge bank account or private family fortunes, no antique dealer goes out of business faster than the one who insists from the onset that they will have only "fine antiques" in their shop—no junk, no collectibles. Shops which have started out like this, if still surviving, do so because they have adjusted their sights to a less pretentious, more realistic view of who their customers are and what the market can supply them on a regular basis.

With some variation in the proportion with which they occur, the component parts of the inventory found in the general-line antique

The inventory of the general-line shop is typically strongest in small household merchandise mixed with collectibles such as toys, quilts, advertising art, primitives, and furniture. View of Missouri Mouse antique shop, 1750 Selby Avenue, St. Paul. (Photo: Rodney A. Schwartz)

store are likely to include some furniture, primitives, an assortment of glassware and china, household textiles, paper goods, comics, toys and dolls, advertising goods, framed popular prints, crockery and kitchen items, jewelry and watches, books, candlesticks, lamps, and rugs. Most shops will also have a few china cabinets of "better" art ware, vases, statuary, and figurines.

Because of the relatively greater breadth of what they offer to the public, the collector here is more likely to find a sleeper or a bargain. Like the collector who does not specialize, the dealer who presents a broad range of merchandise cannot know everything equally well. Like other collectors faced with an attractive bargain, the generalist dealer will buy an item in the hope that it is better than its price. The obvious result of this practice is that some objects whose true value (either aesthetic or monetary) has not been recognized may be found here. A collector may assume that all of these dealers know what a Shirley Temple blue glass pitcher, a 1947 Bing and Grøndahl Christmas plate, a Mickey Mouse wind-up toy, and a wooden coffee grinder are worth. These are all "in the books," with pictures and price quotations for easy comparison. The generalist, however, is less likely to know the difference between an original print and a commercial reproduction, or a print and a drawing, or a paisley and a kashmiri shawl, a period Chippendale chair or a "centennial" piece. These differentiations are subtle, and comparative objects are less likely to be present in readily available source books for positive identification and accurate pricing. For both the collector and dealer, these are the essentials of connoisseurship which are slowly developed, but once possessed they are never lost.

The enlightened dealers are easily recognized by the stock of source books which they keep (and regularly use) in their business. The wise dealers also subscribe to trade newspapers, journals, and other periodicals which serve to continually update them as to prices and trends, and expose them to new avenues of collecting or whose feature articles provide historical background for specialty collecting.

The fact that the general-line antique shop is the most common, and seems to be the least likely to go out of business, is certainly in part attributable to the accessibility of replacement inventory which is plentiful and affordable. It also offers the type of stock which is the most popular to the largest share of the collecting public. The actual percentage of the stock of a general-line antique shop which qualifies as being "antique" even by relatively loose interpretation is not likely to be high. Some local antique dealers' associations, in fact, have attempted, without much success, to require these shops to advertise themselves more honestly as "collectibles" shops or by using some more accurate description of their actual contents. By virtue of an object's relative merits of beauty, handcrafting, and certainly of age, many of the offerings of these shops simply do not qualify as antique. Much of what is for sale in such places can be found in the pages of a 1920s' Sears or Montgomery Ward catalog. This is not to say these items are not worth having or collecting; they just are not antiques. While the specialized dealer, who is usually working with more money, can afford to have things sit longer waiting for the right admirer, the general-line dealers buy what they hope sells quickly, and often it is contrary to any personal taste which they may possess.

An experienced collector does not even have to enter a shop to spot one which offers general-line goods. Signs over the door such as "Calico Cat," "Connie's Corner," "Great Expectations," "Wagon Wheel," "Treasure Trunk," "Remains to be Seen" (better used for a mortuary), "Grandma's Attic," "Country Cousin," "The Red Barn," "Poke and Hope," and other clever monikers are common in the business coast to coast, and betray the homely and generic nature of the contents they hold.

General-line antique shops, because of what they are and who runs them, frequently offer for sale items which are vaguely related or completely unrelated to the antiques themselves. Smaller towns and rural areas often host shops with such odd signage as "Antiques and Gift Shop," "Antiques and Beauty Parlor," and even occasionally "Antiques and Live Bait," or "Antiques and Waterbeds." Sometimes combination shops make sense, such as antiques and furniture upholstering and refinishing, and lamp and clock repair. Shops with a dual purpose are often the products of a husband and wife team, each of whose talents are being exploited. They offer antiques and related services to the collector who needs both.

Those shops that combine antiques and gift items are the most problematic for the naive consumer. For it is here that the blurring of distinction between what is old and what simply *looks* old is the most confusing. Newly produced "country" items made of pine and painted with desaturated blues, rusts, and browns, while stressed and sanded to look old, and other cute things adorned with small-print cotton textiles, are the bane of the serious country or primitive collector. The usual history of stores offering such merchandise is that the new items will become an increasingly large part of the total inventory and, eventually, the antiques will disappear altogether. The reason is simple: it is easier to order new goods for replacement than it is to scout out saleable antiques. Many shops will sell refinishing supplies, metal polish, hand-dipped candles, and other items likely to be in demand by collectors. But beyond the occasional need for such items, the sophisticated antique collector does not like to shop in places like this where new and old are capriciously mixed.

Shops which sell antiques and *reproductions* of antiques side by side are also generally to be avoided. Quality reproductions of furniture, pressed glass, lighting fixtures, coverlets, or counterpanes all have their place—in furniture or department stores, not antique stores. Why would anyone hunting for antiques want a reproduction when the real thing was available? Proprietors of shops who handle reproductions are as much as admitting that they have neither the sources for, nor the money to buy, the real thing. Good reproductions are seldom cheap, and often are similar in price to comparable old pieces because, for one thing, one is paying for modern labor. Sometimes these reproductions are called *newtiques,* a contradictory term if there ever was one, and may be facsimiles of round oak tables, curved-front china cabinets, and ice boxes made into cocktail bars. Reproductions neither hold their value nor appreciate the way antiques do.

Country Shops

Many would-be collectors firmly cling to the odd notion that people in small towns, farmers, and even antique dealers located in rural areas are somehow naive, stupid, and ignorant of the true value of anything. Holding to this illusion, these dreamers imagine that they can drive down gravel roads and find shops filled with fabulous, undiscovered antiquities and, owing to the gullibility of the rustic proprietor, can pick up Windsor chairs, immigrant trunks, and letters signed by Thomas Jefferson for a song. On the rare occasions when this has been true, it becomes the stuff of legends.

Most rural shops, with the notable exception of some in New England which specialize in quality furniture and other early Americana, fall into the category of general-line shops. Aside from having more agricultural paraphernalia, crockery, and the like, they are little different in the inventory they offer than metropolitan shops which have a broad, general line of merchandise. Dealers in rural areas buy locally, and what they have in their shops is representative of what local residents have owned, which may or may not be anything of great value. But because rural dealers also buy at auction, along with everyone else, and even buy in the cities from other dealers, they are well aware of what the wider market brings. The dough box which they proudly show may have been on several dealers' floors before it reached theirs—the price rising with each change of hands. Collectors should never assume that the rural location of a shop means that bargains are automatically theirs or that the sleepy vendor has only straw betweeen the ears.

Consignment Shops

A consignment is merchandise not owned by the dealers, but by someone who has entrusted them with the task of selling it for a percentage of the gross sale. Almost all levels of antique shops will accept consignment items if they are of quality and fit the "image" that the shop generally presents to the public with its own inventory. For the owner of a shop, a certain percentage of consignment items will not only supplement their own stock but, most appealingly, require no outlay of cash for fresh merchandise. There are also consignment shops whose entire stock is exclusively assembled through a consignment process. This is an even more attractive arrangement for the proprietor, whose major expenses then are limited to rent, utilities, and insurance, not in inventory. These shops, however, are seldom solely limited to the selling of antiques and collectibles. Usually they offer a preponderance of newer upholstered furniture and other good, useable furniture a decade or so old, lamps, pictures, and other accessory items of varying ages and quality.

An individual wishing to sell a few items, or a roomful, who does not want to handle the sale personally and hasn't enough to make a house sale worthwhile, may make arrangements with a consignment shop to market the goods. A simple contract is drawn up which usually states the limits of liability for the dealer, and the time period the items are to be held—anywhere from a month to three months. It also states the percentage of profit the dealer will charge, usually 25% to 33%. On especially fine or very expensive items, the dealer may be willing to charge a smaller commission just for the prestige of showing the antique in the shop.

In establishing the appropriate price for a consigned item, the dealer usually asks the consignor what he or she wants to "get out of" the piece. The dealer then adds the percentage of their take, and may make a final adjustment of the selling price based on their own experience with what comparable items sold in their shop have actually brought. This may make the asking price somewhat higher or lower than what the consignor may have initially wanted. Those who consign merchandise for sale do not have the advantage of receiving ready cash for their property which direct selling or even some auctions can accomplish. They have to wait for their money until the item is sold. If the consignment lot consists of more than one item, payment checks to the owners are usually written at the end of each month sales occur. It may take months for owners to be reimbursed for all items consigned. Because the consignment dealer is continually being offered merchandise by the public, the dealer may offer to buy the items immediately for cash. For those who do not want to wait for their profit, this may be a beneficial transaction for both dealer and seller.

Dealers who handle consignments, like any other purveyors of antiques, want a fresh-looking shop and discourage items from sitting on the floor month after month. For the collector it is well to know that consigned items, in order to move them quickly, will often be discounted after the first month they are shown. It is perfectly appropriate for anyone interested in purchasing a consigned item to ask about a discount. Even if the item has not been on the floor long, the dealer may phone the consignor to determine whether or not he or she is willing to take less for the wanted item. A ready customer and the prospect of a quick turnover of merchandise are worth more to a dealer than the few extra dollars of profit which may have resulted from the sale of the item later at a higher price.

Junk Shops and Secondhand Shops

The operators of junk shops seldom refer to their own businesses as such. Junk shops and secondhand shops are at the lowest level of regular retail antique trade. Because their proprietors are often unsophisticated and the least knowledgeable about what they have, the goods they offer are uniformly common. Ordinarily this would be to the advantage of the collector, if the wares they sold were worth having. These dealers are often the least aggressive and competitive in their search for good inventory and really do not need to be. Quite naturally, in the ecology of the antique trade, the least of quality rather automatically falls to them because they are willing to pay the least money for their stock. They are called in to clean up estate sales after a household has been picked over by collector and dealer alike; they haunt garage sales and auctions, buying up box lots of just about anything. They do very little preselecting or editing of merchandise for their shops, where even a brief glance will give the visitor the impression that quantity has been more a consideration than quality.

Run-of-the-mill household goods are the rule in junk shops. Partial sets of anything—the imperfect, the incomplete, the ordinary—are all to be expected. There is little that is pretentious, grand, or even pretty. There is occasionally something that is interesting and rarely something that is good. But since these dealers pay bottom dollar for what they buy and are often the last ones in to do the buying, their likelihood of being left with anything of quality is fairly remote. Knowing how few items of real quality they have, the junk dealer is quite likely, when finding an occasional good piece, to keep the price high, often higher, in fact, than a comparable piece in a better shop. Many experienced antique collectors and dealers looking for treasure feel that searching secondhand shops is not worth the trouble. Others of this same ilk revel in the hope, however slim, that a great find here awaits their critical eye.

Antique Malls and Antique Supermarkets

The most recent development in the antique retail trade is that of the antique mall or antique supermarket. Faced with the soaring costs of everything connected with starting a business, plus the added complications unique to the buying and selling of antiques, many experienced dealers, tired of the responsibility of their own shop, or novice dealers too timid to start one of their own, have chosen to collaborate with other dealers and form cooperative ventures. Ordinarily a dealer, or simply a business entrepreneur, will rent or buy a large building in a good location and sublease spaces to interested parties. The rent, which varies from a hundred or so dollars a month to many hundreds, covers the cost of the use of the space, cleaning and maintenance of the building, light, heat, air conditioning, security, and the ever-mounting costs of hazard and liability insurance. Stall or space rental may also cover the costs of collective advertising in local newspapers, radio, and television. This is a luxury which the independent shop can seldom afford.

Clearly the collaborative system is advantageous to the dealer. For the novice seller it is a good way to test the waters. With a few thousand dollars to invest, the beginner can open a respectable booth of saleable merchandise, with no further commitment of time or money than a six-month or one-year lease. Dealers do not have to manage their booths on a daily basis, thus freeing plenty of time for buying inventory (or having a real second job that pays the bills). The cooperative effort means that dealers take turns in assisting customers and patrolling the aisles when their several days of shop duty arrive each month. A central check-out system, where national credit cards are usually acceptable, takes care of all sales, receipts, and bookkeeping. At the end of the week or month the management writes a check to each dealer for merchandise sold. Like the strips of antique stores along any metropolitan avenue or country road, the consolidation of so much merchandise in a small area assures a considerable flow of customer traffic on a regular basis, much more than most independent shops could hope for.

As in antique shows, the gathering of many vendors together in an antique mall or supermarket causes considerable dealer-to-dealer trading prior to opening to the general public. As virtually every piece of merchandise on the floor will have been previously examined by many of these knowledgeable people, it is unlikely that great undiscovered treasure will be revealed too frequently to the average collector.

For the collector, the antique mall or supermarket is an efficient way to shop for collectibles. The offerings of sometimes 50 to 100 dealers are easily accessible under one roof. If purchases are made from several dealers, a single check is written for the total. Malls of this kind, because they represent the collective efforts of many different dealers, tend to bridge the full range of used goods found in the variety of independent shops mentioned earlier. Malls house the stock of the generalist as well as that of the specialist, from the ordinary and expected to the extraordinary. The variety of goods available in close proximity allows the cautious buyer to compare quality, condition, and price from one stall to another. Many of the dealers who participate in this enterprise do not do it as their sole source of income. Some are former shopkeepers trying to wean themselves of their businesses, others are hobbyists and dabblers who want to keep their fingers in the trade. The person making the most money on this business arrangement is undoubtedly the landlord who is regularly raking in the rent receipts whether or not sales have been brisk.

Flea Markets

The history of flea markets can be traced at least to the Middle Ages when European city and country fairs offered new and used goods, as well as food and produce, to the public with a frenzy of activity and carnival atmosphere. Today, flea markets, or swap meets, as they are referred to in some parts of the country, are a regular component of hundreds of thousands of people's lives, often taking precedence over the usual shopping mall mania, and sometimes even replacing church as a regular Sunday activity. The casual, friendly, bartering atmosphere of the flea market attracts many buyers who would never consider entering a traditional antique shop. It is here that the amateur and the professional buyer alike match their wits with sellers who not only expect a hard bargain but encourage it. In flea markets, prices are almost never firm and seldom high. Sometimes items are unpriced, waiting for an interested party to make an offer; this is the charm of the system which has so many eager participants.

Flea markets are temporary settings for the selling of antiques, collectibles, and general merchandise, promoted and run by people who own, rent, or manage the property on which they are held. Empty lots, grassy fields, parking lots, drive-in theaters, and unheated buildings are likely sites for these events. Stalls are rented to any vendor who has something to sell. Rental on a one- or two-day basis costs anywhere from $5 to $100 or so, depending on the quality of the enterprise and

*At flea markets, expectant collectors who seek quantity
more than quality may have a lot of fun, see a great
variety of merchandise, and, even occasionally, may find
an antique. Urban flea market. (Courtesy of Minneapolis
Star and Tribune)*

the potential for good traffic. Across the country, flea markets vary considerably from the anything-goes swap meet of new, used, and surplus merchandise to the ones limited exclusively to collectibles and antiques. Flea markets are advertised in local papers and in national flea market directories available at larger newsstands. They tend to be set up in the same place and same time each year.

Despite the casual and disorderly appearance of flea markets, many of those who work the stalls are full-time professionals who follow the markets from coast to coast with the seasons. They live out of their vans with the hope (and knowledge) that there are bargains to be had, and that they will get them and find a buyer willing to pay more than they did. Others who participate in flea markets are the occasional junkers who pick up inventory at garage sales and other places, and when they get enough together, they rent a stall. Still others are dealers who have shops, but want to unload lesser merchandise quickly, and some sellers are simply family members trying to clear out their garages and basements. In many states, the stricter tax laws of recent years require sellers to have a tax number and collect state sales tax, and have all but eliminated the amateur seller from this arena, and thus some of the potential for real bargains as well.

Set-up time at flea market is usually 5:30–6:00 a.m. The aggressive buyer will get there as early as the gates open to the public. The best bargains are usually gone within the first hour of opening. The even smarter buyer will set up his or her own stall, and even this early, when only dealers are allowed, can see whatever other dealers are unloading from their vehicles, and may have the first pick of the fresh merchandise. The amount of buyer-to-buyer trading in flea markets is astounding; the wise seller will bring someone else to watch their stuff while making the rounds for further purchases to then mark up and put in their own stall.

In addition to the regular vendors, flea markets are also populated with the familiar faces of collectors and buying dealers who are quite predictable in what they are looking for. After attending or selling at the same flea market a few times, one immediately recognizes the kids who buy beer cans and '50s records or the big man who drives up and down the rows of stalls in his even bigger car, never bothering to get out, who asks for swords and guns and military paraphernalia. There's always someone looking for salt and pepper shakers, baskets, old radios, or rusty tools.

Flea markets are not the places to find period furniture, sterling silver, fine porcelain, great rugs, or art. They are much more likely to provide a setting in which one can find amusement, some serious people-watching, and occasionally something worth having. It is perhaps a better place to sell than to buy. There are always those looking for curiosities and useable household goods who are willing to spend a few dollars for them. Realistically, the kind of treasures one might expect to find here are items which are not valuable because of their magnificent presence, but those sleepers whose true worth has been unrecognized because of their unassuming character. A first edition of a Sinclair Lewis novel, an early Beatles hit record, a hubcap for a '49 Ford, or a simple piece of art pottery with an obscure mark are likely kinds of discoveries waiting to happen at flea markets.

Antique Shows

Temporary exhibitions and sales of antiques known as antique shows can be found at all levels of quality and size throughout the country. Some are the immense nationally advertised auditorium shows in the biggest cities, in which several hundred dealers vend their wares among befuddled customers who carry maps delineating the complex arrangement of stalls, lest they become disoriented. Others run the range from shows of state-wide dealers in the local armory or town hall to the most pathetic, charity-sponsored church basement or school gymnasium sales. In these settings, the number of participants is usually related to quality, though not exclusively. Metropolitan areas regularly

The specializing dealer at an antique show seeks a narrow group of collectors who may be looking specifically for old hunting and fishing gear, toby mugs, depression glass, clocks, jewelry, or dolls. Richard Larson Antiques stall, Minneapolis Auditorium Antique Show (1987). (Photo: Rodney A. Schwartz)

feature large, recurring shows, usually promoted by managers who do this for a living on a national scale.

The largest antique shows, displayed with the wares of several hundred dealers, are a test of the patience, endurance, and discerning eye of the most seasoned collectors. For the amateur, the visual over-load can be overwhelming; it may create confusion, frustration, and fatigue. The advantage for any buyers, who have paid their $2 to $10 entry fee, is that the objects on view represent the combined invento-ries of regional or national dealers who are showing their best goods in

Furniture dealers participating in an antique show need to sell only a few items to turn a profit. Buyers may be paying them for hauling it around the country, but not for steady rent on a shop. Victorian Galleries stall, Minneapolis Auditorium Antique Show (1987). (Photo: Rodney A. Schwartz)

a setting which allows for great efficiency in viewing quality merchandise and even comparison shopping. Many participating dealers will have a specialty and become known among their regular customers as the source for certain kinds of antiques. Some stalls will feature only cut glass, silver, art pottery, postcards, oriental rugs, pressed glass, lamps, prints, toys and dolls, advertising memorabilia, Art Deco, Victorian furniture, pine furniture, country goods, jewelry, clocks and watches, or just about any other category of focus that can be imagined.

Good antique show managers have reputations for creating successful events and are the most likely to attract top-level dealers. Those who participate, and pay the manager anywhere from $100 to $1,000 for a two- or three-day stall rental, are assured that all the invited dealers will have consistently high quality merchandise (no rusty farm implements or old saws with decorative scenes painted on them), which will complement their own inventories. Exhibitors are also especially conscious of how aggressive public advertising will be. The best show managers will promote their events with a multi-media blitz and by mailing reminders to regular customers to ensure the largest and most receptive audience for their dealers.

The largest shows frequently offer services in addition to antiques. Silver and porcelain dealers may participate in "matching services," finding particular patterns of flatware or china for customers needing to complete a set. Others will remove chips from stemware or will provide polishing, repair, and refinishing products and services of all kinds. To the serious and enlightened collector, a visit to the book stall is essential, since it is likely to have a publication on virtually every antique and collectibles topic. Some shows even feature security hardware and alarm systems, and video tape inventory services for the advanced collectors who desire documentation of their antique collection for insurance purposes.

In antique shows, similar and related items offered by several dealers can be compared for quality, condition, and price, thus assuring the best value to the consumer. The prices which are found at antique shows are at least as high as those found in shops. In fact, many of the items are taken directly from a dealer's shop stock, without changing price tags. The prices found in the stalls of exhibitors who exclusively do antique shows and have no shops will generally reflect "national" prices; that is to say, they will have the highest market price found usually on the east or west coast. It is well for the customer to remember that prices at antique shows are seldom firm, and almost any dealer, if asked politely, will agree to a 10% discount, sometimes more. On the last day—and especially the last hour—of a show, a dealer is the most likely to be amenable to price reductions, since fewer items repacked mean an easier trip home, less breakage, and more cash for fresh merchandise.

There are always a certain number of anxious collectors who will line up at the gates of an antique show in order to be the first to enter and seize the bargains. Considering the vast array of merchandise available and the broad variety of interests of individual collectors who are unlikely to want what someone else does, this seems like a phenomenal waste of energy. Actually, what many of these early birds fail to recognize is that the briskest selling and the hottest dealing are done in the hours of set-up time prior to the public's admission when the dealers buy from each other. In these instances, the price of the recently traded merchandise has probably doubled even before the show has opened. For the bargain hunter, shows are generally disappointing. Some antique shows allow nonshowing dealers early admittance by special invitation and higher ticket price to do their buying ahead of the public anxiously awaiting admittance at another gate. Exhibitors who regularly sell at major antique shows and are exposed to the merchandise, expertise, and pricing of other dealers are fairly unlikely to be selling much they do not understand, or at least have not priced correctly.

The disadvantage in shopping for antiques at a show of two- or three-days duration is that decisions need to be made relatively quickly. This is advantageous to the dealer, but for the contemplative collector it means that coming back a week later, or when there is more money in the checking account, is not possible.

Auctions and Their Types

> After lying half a century in his garret and other dust holes these things were not burned. Instead of a bonfire, there was an auction, an increasing of them! The neighbors eagerly collected to view them, bought them all, and carefully transported them home to their garrets and dust holes to lie until their estates are settled, when they will start again.
>
> Henry David Thoreau
> journal entry, upon attending an estate
> auction in New England, 1845

Since classical times, auctions have proved to be one of the best arenas in which to obtain fair market values. Auctions are periodically-held public sales of property sold to the highest bidder by agents who act on behalf of the owners for a commission. The content of an auction may be the exclusive property of a single estate, the combined goods from several estates, or may consist of the possessions of numerous consignors or even merchandise recently purchased by the auctioneer specifically for resale. Much auctioned property is represented as estate merchandise regardless of its actual source; buyers prefer thinking they are bidding on goods which have come directly into the market from a private collection even if they have not. Auctions are either catalogued or not, depending on their content or format. In most auction houses, auctioneers make their profit by taking a commission on the gross sales from both buyer and seller.

Buying at auction is different than buying anywhere else. In shops, estate sales, and even flea markets, it is the *seller* who establishes the general price of an antique. But in an auction, it is the *buyer* who is responsible for determining the final price. This fact alone means that the buyer has a tremendous responsibility for being thoroughly familiar with the merchandise and its value in relationship with the current (or anticipated) market. For the amateur, the auction is the most intimidating and the most dangerous of all places to begin collecting. It requires the surest scrutiny, the quickest eye and hand, and the greatest self-restraint of any antique-buying situation. For the expert, buying at auction can bring the greatest personal satisfaction and monetary reward. It is in this setting that one can exercise the full measure of one's intelligent expertise, business acumen, and timing skill in a room filled with a stimulating mixture of public admirers and hostile combatants. For the antique collector, no victory is sweeter than the one achieved publicly.

Auctions, like antique shops, can be found at all levels of quality and character. The great auction houses of Europe and America are the pacesetters for the remainder of the auction world and the global antique market. Local metropolitan auctions, some good and many worse, sell whatever comes their way. Farm auctions clean out everything not nailed down, including antiques, barns, and cattle. What all auctions have in common is that everything is sold by the end of the scheduled event, and nothing is returnable. A description of the various kinds of auctions will help identify their essential differences.

House and Farm Auctions

In recent years, farm auctions have become all too familiar a sight with the declining profits and rising expenses of maintaining small agricultural businesses. For the better part of two centuries, however, rural auctions in this country have been the standard method for the disposal of property, both personal and real. It is a system, transplanted from

Europe, which is both efficient and fundamentally fair to both buyer and seller. In an auction held on the farmstead, or on the lawn of the house in a small town, the contents of the sale are entirely determined by what the former owners had. And in small towns, many folks make it their business to know what others have and what is worth having. Country auctioneers, whose reputations must be flawless to earn the confidence and generate the future business of local inhabitants, are not likely to "plant" a sale with added merchandise just to spice up the wording of the handbill or bring a momentary high to an otherwise dull event.

Country auctions are usually held at the site of the estate being liquidated, outdoors, or in a large tent or barn if weather is threatening. The contents of the estate are spread out for ease of previewing. Flatbed wagons or the ground are the standard showcases for smaller or boxed merchandise. These events are advertised through local papers, posters, and handbills. All major and many lesser items which the sale contains will be listed as well as the auctioneer's name. Many auctioneers who are amusing and interesting to watch will have developed a devoted corps of followers who, like other locals, will attend auctions whether or not any specific item interests them. Rural auctions are to small towns what Tupperware parties are to larger cities; it is considered in poor taste not to attend and at least buy a "little something" from the auctioned property of an acquaintance. Locals consider auctions social events—a form of entertainment where they meet neighbors, friends, and relatives, and may even find something useful to buy. For out-of-towners, they may offer buying opportunities not found in retail shops.

The percentage of a country auctioneer's commission is dependent upon the amount of work required of him and the quality of the goods being sold. If a family is willing to haul merchandise themselves, the auctioneer will not have to employ such a large set-up crew and may be content with a smaller commission. Usually a charge of between 10% and 25% is standard, less than an auction house in town would charge, primarily because the country auctioneer has no rent to pay, and business overhead is generally lower.

For the auctioning process to be of benefit to the buyer, it is absolutely essential that full advantage be taken of the preview period. In a rural auction, this period usually will be the morning of the actual sale which may begin at 12:00 noon or 1:00 p.m. At a preview, all the goods to be sold that day will be available for inspection by potential buyers. During the auction, in the heat of battle, it is difficult if not impossible to make rational decisions, and merchandise seen across the farmyard can seem momentarily flawless. A wise use of inspection time looking for chips, cracks, repairs, or missing parts prepares the buyer for the field of action when decisions must be made rapidly but sensibly. This is the time to examine the entire contents of miscellaneous box lots. A carton of unmatched dishes may have a rare comic book or a sterling hatpin lining its bottom. It is no one's fault but the buyer's if an auction purchase is an unhappy one or if a bargain is missed.

Potential buyers at auction register in advance with the management just before—or even during—the auction and are assigned a number. This procedure is essential for the seller to keep track of who buys what, and to simplify the process of adding up a customer's bill at the end of the sale. It is also a guarantee that bidders are identified by name, address, and driver's license should a misunderstanding arise during the sale or later when their checks are cashed.

The country auctioneer is, above all, a master of the audience and knows how to play it for the best game and the best profit. To this crowd, an auctioneer will exaggerate, fib, lie, condescend, argue, insult, and even flatter. He will tell stories about the merchandise, disparage it, and praise it. He may tell the buyers they are lucky to get it, or fools to have bid on it. This behavior is expected and acceptable to the audience. The auctioneer's banter may be seductive, enchanting, even hypnotizing, but it is all purposeful, and along with the phrase "Going, going . . . " is planned to squeeze every last dollar out of his clients' goods. One should never believe a word an auctioneer says except "Sold."

Many lower-end auctioneers will use *auction babble*, a personal nomenclature of largely meaningless and often unintelligible words which are repeated endlessly in a rhythmic patter as fill-ins in their monologue. Phrases such as "What'll ya give, what'll give," "Here a dollar," "Gimme a five, five, five" are commonly used, with considerable invention and stylization between various auctioneers.

To warm up the crowd, auctioneers will sell unimportant merchandise first. This usually may be box lots of household junk, rusty carburetors, or a rotting wagon wheel. The selling of these introductory lots allows the uninitiated audience to become familiar with the auctioning process and accustoms the veteran sale goer to the personal style of the auctioneer. It also sets the tempo at which subsequent better goods will be sold and puts the buyers in an urgent frame of mind. An auctioneer's hype, and the artificially brisk pace at which auctions are held, create an atmosphere of tension which is only to the advantage of the seller and to the very experienced buyers who use their wits against someone more timid and indecisive and less certain about what he or she is buying under such pressure.

A good auctioneer will generally open a bid relatively low, probably well less than half of its expected outcome. This entices the entry

The contents of a typical rural auction may include
crockery, tools, machinery, smaller household goods,
furniture, primitives, and rustic items. Sometimes it is
more cheaply gotten than in the city. Rural midwestern
auction during preview period. (Courtesy of Minneapolis
Star and Tribune)

of many early bidders and quick competition among those who think
they are going to get a bargain. The gradual incremental increases of
bidding seem harmless enough at first to the competitors, but soon the
lot has achieved a price equal to—or even greater than—its value. Bidders who never would have considered agreeing to an opening price of
$150 for a Victorian chair frame might easily end up bidding $175 for
the same piece if it started much lower, but where there were several
other eager contestants who forced up its price.

Some lesser auctioneers regularly start opening bids too high.
When no one in the audience is willing to agree to such inflation, he
will have to lower the opening price anyway, sometimes by half, to
encourage entrants. For some amateur auction goers, this practice may
give the false impression that lots are going very low, even disappointing the auctioneer. The technique of using high opening bids will be

used intermittently throughout the sale to reinforce the illusion that the auctioneer is not getting nearly what the things are worth (a fact which he will declare from time to time). No matter how irritating this practice is, it is apparently effective in attracting active bidding by bargain hunters.

The buyer usually bids using a number card which can be more easily seen and recorded by the auctioneer than a hand, a raised eyebrow, or a wink. It is especially dangerous to wave this card absentmindedly, to use it for scratching one's head, fanning against the heat, or swatting flies. Any false move with the card may commit the bearer to an unwanted purchase—an elk's head, a bathtub, or most of the parts to a car engine.

In farm auctions particularly, the percentage of the inventory which is antique is usually relatively small. For the collector this is bad and good news. On the negative side, it means that the problem of searching for antiques here requires the utmost patience in rummaging through irrelevant debris to even identify anything which may be interesting, then waiting for it to be put on the block—a time which is always an uncertainty. On the positive side is the obvious fact that if an auction is attracting potential bidders because of the quantity of farm equipment, tools, and sofa beds being offered, then the lonely antique collector may have very little competition in the bidding.

Because the rural auction is almost never catalogued, the potential buyer has no written description of the items being sold and, worse yet, has no idea when they will be put on the block. In practical terms, this means that those interested in the brass bed, the cobalt-painted crockery, or the box of linens with an eighteenth-century sampler slipped in may have to wait four or five hours for their lots to come up for sale. The auctioneer, of course, uses this uncertainty to advantage; it keeps up the mystery and interest in the entire sale.

Occasionally auctioneers running an uncatalogued sale may be persuaded to offer a lot earlier than planned to accommodate an interested party. More often, they won't be bothered by such suggestions. Despite all external evidence, auctioneers running sales of this kind know much more than their demeanor of casual indifference would suggest.

Quite naturally, good items will be sold toward the end to retain eager customers, though enough better pieces will be sprinkled throughout the sale to keep up the morale as the auctioneer perceives waning attentions or lagging bidding. The uncatalogued sale also means that if a single lot of miscellany such as a box containing jars of nuts and bolts, putty knives, and electrical parts does not bring a bid from the audience, the auctioneer will add an item or two from another lot—a snow shovel or a laundry plunger—to sweeten the pot. In a catalogued auction in a city auction house, this practice would not only be inappropriate, it would be illegal. In sales of this kind the collector often buys what he or she does not want in order to get the one thing in the lot which is of consequence. At the end of such a transaction, it is not unusual that another member of the audience may approach the buyer of a box lot to buy an item from it which the original bidder may not have wanted.

Auction Houses

The term "auction house" is generally reserved for the greatest European auction firms, which have been selling masterpieces of art and decorative arts to royalty, museums, and distinguished collectors since the eighteenth century. Firms such as Christie's and Sotheby's, founded in London, now operate internationally in major capitals such as Amsterdam, Brussels, Geneva, Hong Kong, Madrid, and Rome. The historic Hôtel Drouot in Paris, Bukowski in Zurich, as well as innumerable auction houses in Austria, Germany, and Scandinavia all take their share of their respective national markets as well as the international market. Both Christie's and Sotheby's have locations in New York, as well as regional offices elsewhere in the United States. In these revered houses, an air of formality prevails. The customer is often greeted by a guard, doorman, or an imposing reception area where visitors are expected to make inquiries and purchase catalogs for past, current, or upcoming sales.

Auctions are scheduled months in advance in order to insure a sufficient quantity of related goods to constitute an entire sale, and to allow adequate time to properly catalog the lots. A large house may have one or more sales per day throughout the year, with the auction season running from September through midsummer. Sales are specialized in various areas of collecting. A single auction, for example, may consist entirely of old master paintings, modern masters, drawings, fans, continental furniture, books, vintage wine, furs and jewelry, gold boxes and objects of vertu, ceramics and glass, or watercolors and prints. Some sales are very specialized and attract a narrower but more select audience. Specialties to be offered may include such groupings as Viking swords and suits of armor, lead soldiers and figures, bookbinding tools, Russian and Polish coins, aeronautical art and literature, Royal Doulton and art pottery, tribal art, atlases, maps, and travel books.

The largest auction houses have a roster of auctioneers, one more distinguished looking than another. They dress in somber suits and, for the sale of the greatest masterpieces, wear tuxedos. They speak quietly

The finest treasures from American and European collections are sold through the great auction houses. Even in this intimidating setting, the cautious collector may occasionally find affordable antiques. Christie's London auction room showing price board with bids simultaneously displayed in major foreign currencies. (Courtesy of Christie's)

in clear, succinct tones and exercise the greatest economy of language and restraint of emotions. Their handleless ivory gavel raps one decisive blow to *knock down* a lot. After having successfully knocked down a record-breaking price for a Rembrandt or a Louis XVI *secretaire-à-abbattant,* such a veteran seller might allow himself the slightest smile or a polite "Thank you very much." These auctioneers never discuss the goods they are selling, except to identify the lot number and possibly the name of the object or the artist. Beyond that, any hype is entirely unnecessary, since in any sale of this kind, no interested buyer needs to be educated, reminded, or convinced of the virtue the piece might have.

Auctioneers dealing in the finest merchandise will probably recognize fully half of their audience at any given sale, for it will be populated with regulars. At the time of a successful bid, an assistant will approach any previously unregistered bidder to complete an information card for the record. For major auctions, potential bidders identify themselves to the house beforehand and indicate their intentions, since a stranger off the street is not likely to be viewed with anything but suspicion if bidding on an old master painting when the increments of bid rises are in the £10,000 range.

Auction houses of the top level receive their lots for sale in several ways. The respected name of the house itself is sufficient to attract the public to bring important possessions for inspection of their property and acceptance for an upcoming sale. Christie's, Sotheby's, Phillips, and others employ numerous experts in specialty areas who discreetly meet with potential consignors behind closed doors to examine a piece of family silver, a picture, or a pair of dueling pistols to determine their appropriateness for inclusion in an auction. If they are not suitable the client is dismissed with the kindly advice that "Perhaps you might do better at one of the smaller houses." Thus the distinctive quality levels of antique selling and buying are established from the top downward.

Properties not brought in off the street for consignment to auction are gone after in another way: they are sought out by auction house staff who are continually conferring with owners about selling their objects. Families of means are often willing to part with miscellany unimportant to themselves, but desirable to others, and they are certainly the most disadvantaged upon inheritance, since staggering European death duties frequently necessitate liquidation of personal property for cash. Potential lots for auction can also be acquired by firms who hold *expertise clinics* in cities throughout the world. At such events, experts with various specialties representing Christie's and Sotheby's, for example, will inform members of the public who bring objects for evaluation what their property is likely to realize at auction. Encouraged by high estimates, many owners will assign their objects to the auction house for an upcoming sale. By such a service, these auction houses have generated millions of dollars in sales.

If the property is acceptable for a future sale, the terms of the consignment are clearly set forth orally as well as in written contract. At this time the *commission rate* for the house is explained. This is a sliding scale based on the actual selling price. In order to encourage top-quality consignments, the commission charge is highest on lots that sell for under $1,000; these are charged 25%. On lots sold at higher prices, the rate is proportionately reduced—to 12.5% on items in excess of $15,000. There is frequently a minimum commission on single lots of $35 or so.

The best auction houses have considerable experience to draw upon in determining evaluations of lots, and with superb archives and records of past sales, it is a relatively simple matter to determine a selling-price estimate with some degree of accuracy. Estimates, then, are listed in the catalog or on a separate page, for the buyer's information. Sitting through a few auctions and checking actual sale prices against house estimates renews one's respect for the accuracy of the staff's expertise and solid business acumen. The estimates are traditionally stated as a range, giving a high and low figure (e.g., £250–300). In perhaps fewer than 10% of the sales does the actual price achieved ever vary from these parameters. When it does, the price is almost always higher, sometimes considerably so, often surprising even the auctioneer, though it seldom shows. For the collector, estimates should be used only as a general guideline and should neither be construed as the actual value of the piece nor entirely govern what one is willing to pay. Lots which sell higher or lower than their estimates are neither necessarily overpriced nor a bargain, respectively.

An auction house may also provide direct monetary *appraisals* for a work of art, collections, or the contents of houses. The charge for such a service is usually between 1% and 1.5%, depending on whether the total value is in excess of $50,000 or less, respectively.

At the time of accepting property for an auction, the consignor may be encouraged by the auction house to have a photograph of a consigned object included in the catalog to supplement its obligatory written description. The expense of this procedure is charged to the consignor, and a colored photo in a slick catalog may cost several hundred dollars, though it is considered to be very useful in drawing attention to a lot, thus increasing the possibility of further interest and bidding.

Presale exhibition periods (*previews*) of lots to be auctioned are available for examination by any interested parties usually several days prior to, as well as the morning of, the sale. At the best auction houses, previews are the best places to become familiar with high-quality objects through close-range looking and handling; this is essential to one's visual education and the development of connoisseurship.

The consignor who leaves property at an auction house would be in a precarious position—uncertain, despite the estimates, of what their things would bring—if it were not for the establishment of *reserves*. A reserve is a limit figure given by the consignor of goods below which he or she is not willing to sell the lot. In an auction which is unreserved, the consignor is fated to take what the lot brings, minus the commission, with no recourse for an unsatisfactory price if there are few interested bidders because of a snowstorm, a political assassination, or a world soccer tournament. The reserve, agreed upon jointly by the consignor and the house, protects the consignor, particularly of expensive property, from heavy losses due to an indifferent market.

A reserve figure is confidential information between the house and the consignor and is acted upon by the combined efforts of the auctioneer and the agent for the house, both of whom know which lots are reserved and which are not, and what the reserve limits are. Reserve limits are realistic figures, optimally set at the low end of what a piece should bring. The agent (or *commission bidder*), accompanied by as many as a half-dozen others representing consignors and absentee bidders, sits at a desk positioned to the side, but within sight of the auctioneer. If a Renaissance majolica plate is consigned to auction, subject to the conditions of a reserve of £2,200, the auctioneer will probably begin the bidding at £1,000, and the price will be gradually increased by increments of £100 or £200. If the estimate of £2,200 is met by audience bidding, then the agent does not intervene. But if bidding slows prior to meeting the reserve, the agent, acting on behalf of the consignor, will raise the bid in an attempt to buy back the property for the client. This intervention may work to encourage further audience bidding to the limit of the reserve; if not, then the lot is *withdrawn* for repossession by the owner. The withdrawal of a lot may be announced by the auctioneer, or is simply understood by the audience, which is used to lots not achieving their reserve.

A house *buy in* of aborted lots not achieving their reserve actually costs the consignor money. Auction houses assign a commission of the reserve as the fee for protecting that figure, usually 5%. This means that it would cost the consignor £110 to retrieve his or her property if it did not meet the reserve; still, this is preferable to selling an object considered by both auction house and owner to be worth £2,200 for a mere £1,000, should unenthusiastic bidding cause such a deflated top bid.

The actual process of bidding in the greatest houses is done with neither hands waving in the air nor a Texas cattle-sale yell from the rear of the room. Considerable discretion in the use of subtle and even private signals during the bidding makes it possible for even the most sophisticated auction goers not to realize who is making the bid, even when seated next to them. Incredible as it may seem to the average collector, owners of the greatest private reserves of antiquities and art seldom do their own bidding, and may not even be present for a sale in which they have a keen interest. They either have the house agents bid on their behalf up to their pre-established limit, or they pay a small percentage to another dealer to bid for them, thereby assuring their anonymity. Absentee *telephone bids* are occasionally delivered live during the auction while a house agent at the receiver, acting on the bidder's behalf, communicates the bid to the auctioneer. Mail bids are also acceptable up to several hours prior to the sale.

Those bidding in the room may also protect their identity by prearranged signals to the auctioneer for a particular sale. A gentleman accompanied by his wife, for example, wishing to buy her an exceedingly expensive masterpiece without her knowledge, may arrange with the auctioneer that as long as he is interested in staying in the ring, he will be reading his catalog nonchalantly during the bidding; when no longer willing to stay with the bid he will remove his eyeglasses, a signal that he has stopped bidding. The most commonly used signal, not easily seen even if one stands at the rear of the room, is that a bidder, upon wishing to enter the bidding, will make a subtle upward nod of the head and continue eye contact with the auctioneer until a sideways or downward head motion (with eyes cast in the lap) indicate the bidding has gone too high for that bidder's further interest. A neophyte in the room, unrecognized by the house, may first attract the auctioneer's attention by raising a single finger from the lap. Any gross movement of limbs would be considered unspeakably gauche in circles of such refinement.

The alert auctioneer (and that is the only kind large houses employ) will be aware of the posturing and gesturing of the entire audience of the sometimes several hundred persons before him. A tentative movement of a catalog or a sudden change in position of someone in the room may prompt a polite query from the auctioneer ("Are you in, madam?") to ascertain that person's true intentions. To assist the auctioneer, house agents seated before him will call his attention to bids which he may have overlooked. Other assistants, cloaked in smocks, called *porters*, carry smaller objects to the front of the room for showing to bidders. As a lot is offered, an object too large to be easily moved stays in its preview position and a porter pointing to it says, "Showing here." Auctioneers at the great houses do not beg for bids, but will slow down the pace of rises as the audience slows its interest, then at the last moment of bidding (rather than the "Going, going, gone" of more casual auctions), the auctioneer will usually say, "Any further interest then . . . any further interest? Fair warning; sold."

Unless disallowed earlier, the auctioneer will often announce the successful bidder with a brief phrase such as "Sold to Colnaghi's" or "Sold to Mrs. Williams" at the end of each lot. When claiming purchases after a sale, the buyer will pay for all lots in cash or bank draft (never credit card in the finest establishments) per their total bids, plus a 10% buyer's fee and tax if applicable. It is well for the novice to remember these extra charges when placing bids—that this percentage is part of the real cost of the antique.

Auction Galleries

In the United States, most permanent auction firms doing business from an established location or doing out-of-house auctions may be described as *auction galleries*. Most of these galleries base their general management on the European prototype, though there are some significant differences discussed in the following section. For one thing, the access of American auction galleries to the sheer amount of splendid, early antiques and art available to the houses of Europe is considerably less. Fine American antiquities, however, are preeminent and a plentiful enough supply of quality continental pieces are regularly offered to attract the attention of collectors at all levels.

The quality of merchandise offered in auction galleries varies considerably from the most magnificent to miscellaneous box lots. Smaller but well-known galleries in Boston, Chicago, Houston, Los Angeles, and Philadelphia regularly auction top-level lots of furniture, pictures, silver, porcelain, and jewelry which find their way into public and private collections in this country and, curiously, into collections abroad. These galleries have regularly scheduled auctions of catalog lots. For the buyer at auction galleries, a careful examination of items in the preview showing and a thorough reading of the accompanying descriptions of lots listed in the catalog are both essential for an adequate preparation for the sale itself.

The "Terms and Conditions of Sale" listed in auction gallery catalogs are similar to those of the European auction houses. The written descriptions of each lot, however, vary in their length and utility of information. A typical objective entry might plainly read, "Set of Ten Wedgwood Service Plates; blue leaf scroll with gold enamel rim, 10.25-in. diameter." A more confusing message may be worded, "Ming Dynasty carved jade figural group, museum quality carving especially in the woman figure and the details of her kimono. Base dates to later." A brief analysis of this statement reveals some interesting things. First of all, while "Ming Dynasty" is generally understood to mean a date between 1368 and 1644, the reader is not informed as to whether the piece is indeed Chinese, or if it is Japanese or Korean. Second, the color of the jade, an important factor in determining its quality, is not indicated. Third, the description of the piece as possessing "museum quality carving," especially in certain parts, is contradictory. If a piece was of museum quality it would be consistently carved throughout. In any case, "Museum quality" is a term of dubious value in this setting; it would be unthinkable, for example, that an artifact actually worthy of a museum, such as a Rembrandt painting, or a Paul de Lamerie wine cistern, would ever be so described anyway. Lastly, "base dates to later" is a helpful, if not complete, warning that the base is not original but is a modern replacement (and, therefore, *not* museum quality). Catalog descriptions may or may not be useful, and, like the auctioneer's own words, they should never be depended upon as substitutes for a thorough personal inspection of the goods prior to bidding.

Bidding is usually done with a numbered card; absentee bids as well as telephone bids are generally acceptable.

Travelling Auction Galleries

Some auction galleries with home bases in large cities will conduct a substantial portion of their business "on the road." They move their inventory from city to city and earn their reputations by promoting their auctions as the estate property of movie stars and other prominent figures, living or dead. In reality, these travelling sideshows disguised as auctions have an air of familiarity about them regardless of whose "estate" is being sold. Whether supposedly owned by a film idol, politician, or other celebrity, the goods are nearly always the same: good (though newer) oriental rugs; some second-rate European paintings; lots of Orientalia, including jade, porcelain, and bronze; and plenty of ormolu-mounted and inlaid furniture. The inventories of these sales are similar to what one might find in the plush shops of the "doorbell dealers."

The examination of a catalog, or attendance at the sale of hundreds of lots, will reveal that its contents consist of relatively little property actually owned by the celebrity whose name is promoted in connection with it. A few dozen lots of jewelry, or small personal curiosities, or even bags of unopened fan mail, are usually the only star-related goods anyone patient enough to sit through the ordeal is likely to be offered. The cautious customer is then reminded that the catalog title (in much smaller print than that of the star's name) also said, " . . . and other major estates and private collections." The private collection most obviously on view is that of the gallery owner who has bought up quantities of flashy, generally newer merchandise—thus the sameness of its appearance from one auction to another—and is hawking it about the country from one naive audience to another.

These auctions are inevitably contrived, despite the management's efforts to make them appear spontaneous and good entertainment. The crowd is sprinkled with *stooges, plants,* or *shills* for the house who are anonymously bidding neither for an absent buyer nor against a reserve, but are buying back merchandise owned by the house which does not achieve a profitable margin from its wholesale purchase price. Unsold goods simply are shipped to the next city to try out on a different audience who may be willing to pay more for them. To maintain an interest to those attending any given sale, the items scheduled in the catalog, which may include as many as 800 or 900 lots, will be offered only upon the request of those present. For this purpose, *request slips* are filled out prior to a sale by any interested party. In this way, not all cataloged items will be put on the block, nor will auctioned items necessarily be in numerical sequence.

Moveable auctions are best suited for collectors who are prepared to pay retail prices for merchandise in good condition—though not necessarily old—within an auction format. For the serious collector who holds the hope of discovery, they are almost always a disappointment.

Mail and Telephone Auctions

The auction whose format is the most unfamiliar to the beginning antique collector is the mail or telephone auction. These differ from all other auctions in that there is no actual sale which takes place at a designated time and location with assembled customers bidding on merchandise which they have all inspected. In absentee auctions of this sort, an inventory of antiques, frequently related by subject, such as early American pressed glass, Russian porcelain, or rare stamps or books, are assembled by a dealer, who then publishes an illustrated and descriptive catalog of the items, sends it to interested parties, and waits for bids to come in from buyers who are bidding blindly. This technique is used mostly by vendors of quite specialized material catering to fairly sophisticated buyers who are more likely to know what they are bidding on from a written description and a fuzzy black-and-white photocopied image. Beginning collectors, should they even be aware of such sales, ought to stay clear of them entirely because they have not inspected the merchandise personally nor have they any sense of what the things are worth from the bidding of others whom they cannot see.

At the time catalogs are distributed nationwide, the deadline for bids is established. Conditions of sale are similar to other auction houses, with the notable exception that a ten-day approval period beyond the date of purchase of the unseen merchandise is allowed—the only auction setting where this is true. When all mail or phone bids have been received, the management reviews the bids after the deadline, and each lot is awarded to the highest bidder. However, the competition for lots may not stop here. Regular users of this service, particularly busy private collectors, or dealers who cannot travel across the country to regularly preview merchandise personally in such events, will alert the management that should any bid top theirs, they would like to be notified and have the chance to outbid the earlier high bid. In these cases, a flurry of long-distance telephone calls from the dealer, often into the early hours of the morning, will keep interested parties apprised of the competitive bids, outbidding each other until the competition drops out. If the management is honest, phone and mail auctions may be a service to some; if not, they can be a horrible scam. The word-of-mouth reputation of such firms from satisfied buyers is essential information before participation in such a sale may be considered safe.

General-line Auction Galleries

For many antique collectors and dealers who want a challenge, a bargain, and the occasional victory of a great find, the general-line auction gallery offers considerable potential. These galleries are found with some regularity throughout the country, usually in larger metropolitan areas, and are an important link in the ecological chain which supplies the general-line antique dealer who may heavily depend on them as a predictable source of inventory. If dealers regularly attend auctions, it is reasonable to assume that the goods they buy there are worth having and are being had at more-or-less wholesale prices. Private collectors have a particular advantage in this setting because they are frequently bidding against interested dealers who need to turn a profit on what they buy. If a dozen cut-glass goblets were offered at auction, for example, a dealer who calculated they could sell in the shop for $150 should pay no more than $75 for them. Thus the private collector intending to keep them would happily outbid the dealer with an $85 offer—$65 less than an ideal shop price.

Any auction, of course, requires only two bidders interested in the same merchandise to create a lively contest. But, like horse racing, it is the difference of opinion which makes one bidder successful and the other not. To a dealer, any given object is worth only 50% of its retail shop price, but if two private collectors are bidding against one another, the fight might be a more heated one, since their appraisals of the contested object are more likely to be higher and they are less apt to be tempered with a businessman's objectivity.

Most general-line auction galleries conduct unreserved sales in which merchandise is sold to the highest bidder regardless of what that bid may be. The unpredictable nature of this arrangement adds excitement to the sale and encourages the hope in those participating that bad weather, a holiday, or an otherwise uninteresting sale will dissuade customers from attending and finding the one treasure they want for themselves. Unreserved sales are appealing to collectors because they are assured that neither the house nor the consignor has set an arbitrarily high reserve which prevents them from buying the antique directly and fairly from an audience which may have less interest in the lot. With the few exceptions of those items specifically prohibited from resale by law, such as machine guns, relics of endangered animals, and used mattresses, these auction houses will also accept virtually any consignment that comes to their door. It might be an outboard motor, a box of leftover garage-sale items, a bicycle, an electronic organ, a well-used sectional sofa, or someone's bad craft projects. This list may not seem encouraging to the sophisticated collector, but it is only a partial one. While the great international auction houses can be very particular about what they accept for sales, smaller local galleries cannot, lest they discourage those who have quality items for consignment (but who also want to dump lesser lots) from doing business with them.

Auction galleries receive a variety of merchandise from many sources to form a single sale. Aside from the easily gotten lesser goods which auction galleries regularly sell, their inventories consist of many other antique and collectible items. Antique dealers will often consign inventory which has sat too long in their shops, or will do so to generate cash for buying fresh merchandise. The unsold residue of estate sales is often sent to auction. Collectors also sell through auction as they upgrade quality or move to new areas of interest. The household goods of an entire estate for which a sale on the premises is not practicable may be auctioned, extensive lots sometimes being divided among several sales. People who are moving out of town, those making plans for their more condensed retirement living, or simply those in need of cash will consign their property to a gallery. The remarkable conglomeration of new, used, and antique goods found in these auctions is matched only by the incongruous composition of those who assemble to bid on it.

Like the greatest auction houses which use a sliding scale for their commission, general-line auctioneers also vary the percentage of the commission to encourage better consignments. A typical schedule might be a 25% to 33% commission on all items whose sale price is less than $100, plus a one- or two-dollar charge on each lot. On sales of lots over $100, a 10% fee plus $10 per lot is assessed to the consignor. A vendor whose roll-top desk brought a hammer price of $850 would thus pay $95 to the gallery for selling it. These galleries also charge a 10% buyer's fee, will charge for pick up and delivery of goods, and may have a fee for reserved seats or for catalogs. On any given auction, the gallery is taking a minimum of 35% commission on the total hammer prices of the auctioned lots.

Collectors planning to bid on lots are generally required to register in advance and receive a bidding card whose number becomes their identification for the house. When the auctioneer begins the bidding by calling out a figure, it means that anyone who raises his or her card is agreeing to that price. So, in effect, the price quoted by the auctioneer is always an increment ahead of what the last agreed-to bid by the audience has been. In the heat of an auction this might become confusing. Occasionally less experienced bidders, hearing the auctioneer ask for a price higher than what they just bid, may confuse it with an actual bid and, in fact, follow their own bid with one higher. An alert (and honest) auctioneer will be aware of the possibility of such bidding against oneself and will call it to the bidder's attention by some such phrase as "You're $50, I need $60," pointing to the embarrassed amateur.

It has often been said that an experienced bidder is never the first to bid, because they may also be the last. This means that if an auctioneer begins the bidding by asking $50 for a worn Oriental rug, and

The preview period of a general-line auction prior to the sale itself is an important time to carefully examine the objects being offered to determine their quality and condition. Rose Galleries, 1123 West County Road B, Roseville, Minnesota, during preview period. (Courtesy of Jerry Kaufhold)

someone immediately raises his or her card in agreement to that price, there is the possibility that there are no other parties willing to pay more, and thus the first bid entered *is* the last; the first bidder may have paid more than would have been necessary had the auctioneer been forced by lack of immediate interest to lower the first request to, say, $25. While being the first bidder should be discouraged, it is important to be an early bidder if entering the contest. Because of the number of lots offered in a single sale, auction galleries often keep a very rapid pace to the bidding, as many as 150 lots per hour, which leaves little time for drawn-out begging by the auctioneer, or contemplation by the prospective buyer. An early bid means that the auctioneer has a chance to notice the bidder's interest, and keeps an eye on them. Those who enter too late run the danger of having the lot knocked down before

Auctioneers move quickly, selling several lots per minute. Both buyer and seller need to be aware of each other's signals and methods of operation to prevent trouble in the heat of battle. Rose Galleries during bidding. (Photo: Rodney A. Schwartz)

they are recognized, thus losing their chance to participate in the contest.

   Absentee bidding is a service provided by all auction houses and galleries, though usually not rural auctions where speed and closure within the day are desirable. Bidding by the absentee method means that anyone interested in one or several lots, but not in sitting through the sale of the 650 miscellaneous items which may compose a single auction, can leave a written bid which will be executed by the house against others on the floor. Usually this service is free, as are telephone bids, though sometimes there is a nominal charge of a dollar or two. If a potential buyer wants an Art Nouveau porcelain vase and is willing to pay $250 for it, a written bid is left for that amount. If, during the actual sale, bidding on the floor goes no higher than $180, then the absentee bidder wins the lot for the next higher increment, or $190 (if $10 raises are being used). In the case of tie absentee bids, the earliest bid to be received is the winner.

   Absentee bids are used for several purposes. Both dealers and collectors who wish to keep the knowledge of their successful bids private will use this system. In some cases, the successful bidder, appearing uninterested, may actually be in the room during the sale but, wishing to remain anonymous, has the house do the bidding. Others use the absentee method as a way of guarding themselves against the entrapment of passionate overbidding, which may occur in any auction. Many absentee bids are left by people too busy or too impatient to sit through hundreds of uninteresting lots for the chance to bid on the one they want.

   To prevent overbidding, it is well for the collector to take a lesson from the dealers who buy at auction. Knowing almost precisely what they will be able to get for the item in their shop, they set for themselves a very firm price beyond which they will not bid. Collectors need to set their own limits before a sale and resolve not to violate them. If an obscurely signed painting which looks like it might be a Hudson River School piece is on the block, it is easy enough to set a limit for oneself of $650, given the oil's condition and the uncertainty of its authorship. But as the bidding goes to $750, it is equally simple to suddenly reassess the value of the picture (which, after all, you were clever enough to recognize the quality of in the first place) because of the surprising interest it is generating on the floor. With incremental rises of $50, it doesn't take long for a picture first thought to be firmly worth $650 to magically increase a hundred or two in the mind of the bidder embroiled in the process as the competition gets stiffer.

   A typical general-line auction house will very simply catalog the lots with no lengthy descriptions. Such a document may read thus:

203. Box of frames
204. 4 cut-glass finger bowls (× 4)
205. Signed landscape painting
206. Round 42" oak table, 2 leaves
207. Early Hummel figure (some chips)
208. Handmade Oriental rug, 4'×6'
209. Box of miscellaneous silver plate
210. Carved soapstone vase
211. 3 unmatched sidechairs, as is (lot)

For the auction goer, a catalog of this kind is useful only for keeping track of the sequence of bidding and what lot is coming up next. Occasionally descriptions will point out flaws in merchandise if noticed by the management, but are otherwise incomplete when mentioning the particulars of the age, origin, or quality of a given lot.

Occasionally in an auction, a lot consisting of several or many related items is sold at the bid *times* the number of articles in the lot. This is clearly stated in the catalog as (× 2) or (× 12). A set of 60 pieces of sterling flatware in the Grand Baroque pattern, for example, might be sold for $15 to $20 apiece × 60. When pairs of items are sold—vases, tables, candlesticks—they are also offered at the bidding price times two. Even if announced by the auctioneer, bidders are sometimes unaware of this arrangement, and they may be surprised that they have just paid double for what they thought was the price of both.

The marketing of antiques and collectibles in an auction follows the same general rules as it does elsewhere in the retail trade. Keeping the customers interested, giving them variety, hyping the sale, and making them think they are getting a bargain are all effective measures to insure their attention. The intensity of pace and the direct participation of the audience are both important factors in making this marketing scheme work. Equally important is the sequence with which merchandise is offered. The auctioneer, or cataloguer of the lots, must be skilled at creating a pace for the sale by the sequencing of lots for maximum effect. The first dozen or so warm-up lots will usually be lesser items. As the auction proceeds, lots will be arranged to create strong interest, action, and high prices intermittently throughout the sale. If a large collection of mantle clocks, music boxes, or Christmas plates are being sold, for example, they are best spread out in groups of four or five over several hours, thereby forcing those interested only in those specialties to stay for the entire auction. Encouraging steady attendance throughout a sale allows more potential bidders; there is little more disappointing to an auctioneer or to a consignor than a nearly empty house created by the trailing interest of bidders who have left because all the good lots have been sold. For a collector or dealer, the tail end of a sale with few competitors left in the audience may be just the opportunity to make profitable purchases.

In the selling of the greatest objects of art and decorative arts, and the disposal of renowned estates—house and land included—the auction is chosen as the preferred method of sale. The reasons are several. The relative speed with which such a transaction can be accomplished makes it a natural choice. More important, public auction is generally considered to be the fairest method for realizing the true market value of any property. If one assumes the auction floor is populated with knowledgeable and interested customers, this concept holds true. At auction, however, like any other place where antiques are sold, a single object has no single price. Its value is dependent on its audience and, in an auction, upon who is present, interested, and doing the bidding. Auctioneers know only too well that a sectional book case might sell for $425 one week and an identical piece, sold at the same auction house several weeks later, might bring only $300. It is equally disturbing that in the same auction where a dealer or collector may be both buying and selling, the prices others are paying seem so small, whereas the ones they have to pay appear inflated.

If anyone in the antique business has an objective and realistic perception of the market value of antiques, it is the auctioneer or the regular auction goer who, week after week, year after year, sees prices hammered down to the person willing to pay the most for them.

Mail Order

DIRECTLY FROM CANTON

A Quantity of Nankeens, at the New York price by package, single as low as any are selling; Bamboo fans, by dozens or hundred; 15 boxes China Tea Sets, containing 45 pieces in a box . . . Platters, Dishes, Plates, Butter Boats, Mustards, Peppers, Pitchers, Mugs . . . Color'd Sattins, Twill'd Black Sattin, Striped Silk . . . and a general assortment of almost every sort of Dry Good

Early nineteenth-century newspaper
advertisement, Hartford, Connecticut

The affection for buying merchandise through the mail has a history which began in colonial times, when the most fashionable and prosperous of our nation's citizens had to depend upon English and continental sources for their stylish worldly goods. Self-conscious early Americans were consumed with a desire to be up to date with European fashion and were frustrated by the dearth of fine domestic goods available to them. Before the Revolution, and certainly afterward, many of the finest furnishings in American homes came from European and other sources. Bolts of silk and cotton yardage for draperies and upholstery, fancy glass and mirrors, and thousands of crates of Chinese porcelain came by shipload to the new nation. Ordered sight unseen by mail, the arrival of new shipments was always the cause of much interest and celebration.

By the late eighteenth century, Westerners were having an influence on what the Chinese actually produced. Mugs, butter boats, salts, and other specialized forms, not originally Chinese, were being requested in increasing quantity by Americans and Englishmen who sent them models of how these pieces were to look. Americans were also sending drawn or engraved coats of arms to Chinese potters who obligingly copied them onto the glazed porcelain which they ordered.

The expansion of the population and the westward growth of American cities prompted a great dependence on ordering by mail. By the mid-nineteenth century, every manner of goods were available in quantity in the east. Sears and Roebuck's mail-order business, whose first catalog of 200 pages was issued in 1893 and advertised products of every sort to the hinterlands, became an American institution. By 1908 their catalog contained 1,184 pages of fabulous products and was a veritable "wish book" for city and country dwellers alike. Each new issue was a delight, and each old copy went "out back" to fulfill an even more necessary function.

Today, ordering anything by mail is big business, and ordering antiques in this way is a flourishing trade. Every antique periodical and trade journal contains advertisements which encourage mail (and phone) communication with dealers. Journals such as *The Antique Trader, Collector's News*, and *Antiques and Collecting Hobbies* are specifically for the purpose of putting collectors or dealers in touch with other dealers who have what they want. At least theoretically, running an antique business by mail is the best of all worlds. It can be done from one's home with minimum overhead, and most of one's capital can be spent on developing an attractive inventory and on advertising. Following the ads of mail-order dealers for more than a year or two, however, will alert the collector to the fact that many, even most, who enter the business will fall by the wayside within a year.

Antique collectors are well advised to peruse the periodicals in which antiques are advertised, to see which dealers are constant participants, and even if they have no intention of buying by mail, it is a good way to keep up with collecting and price trends which may not be the same as the more familiar local ones. Because of the costs of advertising (often as much as $10–$15 per column inch), most dealers specializing in mail order will only handle those items which, in clear profit, are worth advertising, insuring, and packing. Because of the modest profits realized by such goods, quantities of general-line antiques priced under $25 are not likely to be found by collectors through the mail. Ordinary household collectibles are better (and more cheaply) bought closer to home.

The merchandise which mail-order dealers stock is perhaps most similar to what might be found in *specialty* antique shops. They will handle better-quality porcelain, glass, and silver, as well as items which are familiar to buyers, such as advertising art or pattern glass. For instance, many highly successful flatware- and china-matching services operate exclusively by mail. Most mail-order dealers will handle only things that are in good condition, and will also offer a ten-day return policy if merchandise does not meet a buyer's expectations. When receiving an order, cautious dealers often send a card which states that delivery will take place in two weeks; this allows time for checks to clear. There are few federal, state, or municipal laws governing the running of a mail-order business with the exception of those involving deliberate fraud. In the purchase of antiques by mail, the collector is denied the thrill of discovery, the personal inspection of the goods, and the possibility to negotiate price with the dealer. For those collectors looking for items to fill in a specialized collection, mail order might well provide an avenue of success.

Estate Sales

> A living man who suddenly parts with his
> collection is inevitably under suspicion; are the
> things fakes? Or is he perhaps just speculating?
> With a dead man's goods, no such question
> arises; they smell right. They are the portion of
> the quarry which is thrown to the hounds at the
> end of the hunt.
>
> Maurice Rheims
> *The Glorious Obsession*

If discovery and the possibility of discovery are the most important factors which keep the antique collector going, then the estate sale is certainly primary of all of the settings to search for treasure. For it is here that one views en masse the possessions of a person's or a family's life. In a properly conducted estate sale, the contents of the home are presented without substantial editing, and without the intercession of a dealer's taste or preselection.

The term "estate sale" is applied quite broadly in contemporary usage, broadly enough, in fact, that many customers are disappointed when entering such a sale to discover that it does not meet their expectations of what they believe a true estate sale to be. Webster's Seventh New Collegiate Dictionary defines "estate" as " . . . the degree, quality, nature and extent of one's interest in land or other property," and in further definition as " . . . the assets and liabilities left by a person at death." Thus an estate is quite simply all the property of an individual whether that person is living or dead. Interestingly, in Denmark, the word used for "estate" is *dodsbo*, which literally means "house of the dead." In this country, the popular usage of "estate" is so often seen in advertisements of such a sale because it has a mystery and romance connected with it which makes the event more marketable than another name. Usually "estate sale" implies that the house will contain the entirety of someone's possessions whether that person is dead or has been moved to a nursing home.

The term "moving sale," on the other hand, more generally implies that the contents are fewer, and are principally those less desirable items that a family has found not good enough, too inconvenient, or too costly to move to their new home. In a typical moving sale one would expect to find bulky items such as upholstered furniture, excess bedroom sets, yard equipment, tools, sporting goods, and other items discarded for a simpler living style or a change of family status. Not a few of these events billed as moving sales are, in fact, divorce sales which in content do not differ substantially from the former.

Seldom do either moving sales or divorce sales contain antiques, for antiques are precisely the things which most people in charge of their own faculties will retain until their deaths. Many a disappointed comment has been overheard at these sales which have been inaccurately billed as estate sales. They indicate that the majority of buyers in this setting expect everything but the body of the deceased to be displayed. These are the same folks who, not finding closets of out-of-date clothes, grocery bags of cancelled checks, half boxes of laundry detergent, bottles of nails and screws, jars of brown fruit canned in 1947, and old dentures, will quickly claim that the sale is not genuine and that it suspiciously reeks of either a "plant" (that many items have been brought in from elsewhere) or, even worse, it has been previously picked over by greedy relatives or even greedier antique dealers.

By general usage then, in a legitimate sale billed as an estate sale, one would expect to find a house or apartment looking more or less like the owners had just left on a vacation with everything in place and everything priced for sale. If eliminating the middle man is the most economical way to buy anything, then the estate sale is one of the best places to purchase antiques directly from the collector—not picked over or doubled in price by a dealer.

How Estate Sales Are Conducted

When a family or a legal agent such as an attorney or banker wishes to have an estate sale conducted it is usually for the purpose of disposing of the entire personal property of its former owner with neatness and dispatch. While the preliminary negotiations and set-up time may entail some weeks or even months, the event itself is usually over in a couple of days. The relative speed of this procedure is of considerable benefit to the efficient settling of the terms of a trust or will, or in generating financial liquidity for a family needing cash for hospitalization or nursing home care, for example. Estate sales are generally conducted in one of two ways. Either they are accomplished by the family of the owner of the goods, or by a professional in the business who is called in to manage the entire event.

Estate sales are not found in all parts of the country and they are virtually unknown in Europe, where estates are almostly always settled through the auctioning of goods. With some exceptions, they tend to be most prevalent in larger metropolitan areas. In the several largest American cities, as in most of western Europe, entire estates are most often liquidated at auction. In these instances, the auctioneer will move the goods to his showrooms and sell it on the block. These sales, interestingly, are still referred to as "estate sales" by the auction house.

Who Does Them

Families who attempt to run an estate sale themselves are often surprised by the amount of both physical and mental labor which such an enterprise entails. Because they are relatives, they frequently lack the objectivity which is required in the successful marketing of used goods. On the one hand, sentiment toward a favorite object may cause them to set an unrealistically high price. Ignorance of true market value, on the other hand, may let a treasure slip by for a pittance.

For these reasons, the collector will find such family-run sales both frustrating and rewarding. Often families involved in such an enterprise are encouraged by someone among their ranks to "save money" by hiring not a professional but someone who may have a passing familiarity with the process of garage and house sales. The buyer looking for paper goods, advertising brochures, postcards, or old magazines may easily walk away with an armful of bargains priced by a relative who has viewed them as trash. Many hardened estate sale goers begin their search of the estate by looking behind the garage where the "unsaleable" trash, discarded before the sale, is waiting for the garbage collector. A less lucky buyer may be overwhelmed by the exaggerated evaluation of an item which the family knew was an antique, such as a brass bed, oriental rug, or mantle clock on which they expected to make a killing.

A simple reading of the want ad for an estate sale usually reveals whether or not the sale is family run. Nearly all professionals will have their name prominently displayed in the ad. This practice both encourages loyal customers to return to buy and recruits new estate sales as well.

Professionally conducted estate sales are run either by people whose sole business is the management of such affairs, or by antique dealers who are otherwise proprietors of shops and have house sales as a supplement to their store-front enterprises. For the latter, it is an effective way to generate considerable cash flow in their bank accounts, keeping their own bankers mindful of their business health and "traffic" potential. Occasionally professional appraisers who are not antique dealers will accept a sale. For the exclusive estate sale conductor, the dealer who does it part time, or the appraiser, the process of finding, organizing, and doing sales is essentially the same.

Choosing the right person to conduct an estate sale is a very serious business. It must be based entirely on a mutual trust for both their expertise and their honesty. They will have keys to the house and access to everything in it. A client must know that their integrity is such that if the sale conductors find money in a suit pocket or a forgotten diamond in a dresser drawer, it will be recognized and dealt with responsibly. Ignorance on the part of a conductor can be as devastating to a client as dishonesty. A string of genuine pearls incorrectly identified and sold as costume jewelry steals from the trusting client as surely as if it had been a cash robbery. The buyer at an estate sale, however, only lives in the hope of this actually happening. At this stage of the enterprise, no one worries about honesty.

Dealers with shops are in a natural position to hear about potential estate business. Drop-in traffic will often lead to a sale, word-of-mouth commentary in neighborhoods where they have conducted other sales to more. Families who see their advertisement in the *Yellow Pages* or in the local paper will call them for assistance. All persons serious about generating estate sale business will have connections with churches, nursing homes, retirement condominiums, and especially bankers and attorneys whose specialty is the settling of trust and estate accounts. These groups are privy to timely information about life changes that may require the services of an estate sale agent. Ultimately the best guarantee for further business is the reputation the conductor has earned by setting up consistently clean, attractive, well-priced, and interesting sales. Loyal followers attend all these sales because they can depend on a certain level of quality goods and fair pricing.

Reviewing the Goods

In a typical scenario, the estate sale professional will be called in to take a look at the contents of a house. At this time the conditions and terms of the sale are established by mutual agreement of both parties. If relatives are allowed to go through and pick favorite objects, that is determined in advance. This can often be the critical stage in which the dealer will decide whether or not to take the sale. If the contents of the home are too few or undistinguished, it may not be worth the time. If so-called "leader" items of antiques and other desirables are skimmed off first by family, the same conclusion may be reached. Not infrequently a dealer who also has a shop (and merchandise waiting to be sold) may contract to do a smaller sale with the agreement that his or her own shop merchandise might be added in to the estate to round out missing furnishings. This is called *planting* or *seeding* a sale, and is frowned on by customers and the purists in the business who will neither add nor subtract from the original contents of the household.

Within minutes of viewing the interior, an experienced estate sale specialist can determine the gross amount which the contents of the home are likely to bring. This is accomplished by quickly adding up low estimates of significant items in the house. The sale price of major furniture, newer major appliances, good rugs, pictures, important collectibles, and antiquities will be totalled. The sophisticated conductor will display a low-key interest in whatever the house holds. Many an amateur, in showing wild enthusiasm for a Tiffany lamp or eighteenth-century highboy has inadvertently given an appraisal to a greedy relative while carelessly mentioning what price they might bring in the sale. Contents of the kitchen, basement, garage, and sometimes the attic are seldom considered in this rough total. This working sum, once established, is generally not shared with the seller of the goods. On the basis of this estimate and by judging the time the sale will take to set up, a simple contract will be signed which sets the terms and date of the sale and the percentage of dealer's profit, and allows for a separate billing for the cost of advertising in local papers which is borne by the owner of the goods. The conductor will guarantee a empty house, swept clean, at the end of the sale period.

The services of managing an estate sale by a professional generally cost the owners of the goods or their agents between 25% and 35% of the total amount taken in from the sale. Occasionally where extensive handling of the merchandise by staff is significant or much preparatory cleaning of the premises is required, a higher percentage may be quoted, even as much as 50% in homes where people have lived like swine. Rarely will an estate sale be conducted for a smaller percentage than 25%, unless the merchandise is of such quality or reputation that a smaller cut of a much larger gross would provide a satisfactory profit for the conductor.

Few dealers want to run a sale with low-end merchandise and even fewer relish the idea of spending a week cleaning out debris and washing every piece of glassware and every toaster before it can be respectably offered for sale. Dealers make their profit from a sale in one of two ways: either because the merchandise is good, expensive, and desirable, in which case the percentage of their take is based on a higher gross amount; or given a small sale with useful though less spectacular merchandise, the contents of the house are clean and organized and require relatively little multiple handling on the part of the set-up staff. Estates which contain hundreds or even thousands of small items, each of which needs separate pricing, cost the dealer considerable hourly wages paid to the crew doing the work. It takes far less time, for example, to price a dining room set or a grand piano, which will bring a fine profit to the dealer and the owner, than to price a bedroom full of miscellaneous linens, shoe stretchers, and bundles of coat hangers, which will bring relatively little. In this business time is definitely money.

Setting Up a Sale

Setting up an estate sale is a labor-intensive task, an effort which to many observers of the finished product is all but invisible. The average two- or three-bedroom bungalow typically generating $4,000 to $5,000 in gross sales will usually take two or three people the better part of a work week to set up. If the dealer receives $1,000 to $1,250 for doing the work, the staff must obviously be paid a minimum wage. Setting up, nevertheless, involves the work of a knowledgeable if underpaid staff, each member of which is able to contribute some specialty. They review the goods and organize them in a manner which brings the greatest clarity to the buyer, and shows the merchandise in the most flattering setting.

All saleable items are removed from inaccessible places such as closets, attics, cupboards, drawers, and other storage areas; the contents of all furniture are emptied. Unless there is enough potentially profitable merchandise in the garage to warrant paying a salesperson two days' wages to watch the stuff during the public sale, these items are frequently condensed into the basement goods. In good weather bulky items such as yard equipment, hammocks, tents, and lawn furniture are displayed outside. Inside, tables are set up everywhere to display glassware, china, and collectibles. Linens are placed on beds, better quilts and tablecloths are shown on coat hangers. Similar and related goods are grouped together for ease of viewing. Any customer having attended more than a handful of sales will know that he or she can always expect to find the most important things in the living and dining room, tools and garden equipment in the basement.

A good estate sale conductor will also clean up debris, hide anything that is not for sale, and not offer to the public any personal items which might compromise the privacy or reputation of their former owners. Efficiency of set-up demands that virtually no time is spent arranging merchandise that will bring no profit but nevertheless must be sold. Washing perfect sets of cut glass goblets is a reasonable investment of labor, whereas sorting National Geographics by date is not, since, except in rare instances, their only real value is to the junk man who is paid to haul them away for pulp. Odd glassware, electrical parts, paperback books, and rusty screwdrivers are usually grouped together unpriced, and offered as "Your Choice, 25 cents."

Pricing the contents of the estate is traditionally done the last day of the set-up, when order has been accomplished and the family has vacated the premises. Pricing done too early attracts the attention of owners still scurrying about anxious to know what their family's possessions are worth. Should this happen, they are invariably amazed at how high the prices are, or equally shocked by how little some things bring. Keeping owners and other interested outsiders away from the property during the organization of the sale (as well as during the sale itself) is a herculean task which requires the persistence of a used-car salesman and the tact of a funeral director.

The pricing found in an estate sale is generally less than that found in an antique shop and frequently low enough that antique dealers performing a 100% markup can still find stock for their business. The fairest pricing is achieved when two pricers work together acting as a check against one another. Experienced pricers know precisely what the market will bear for most ordinary household goods. Used food mixers, snow shovels, Ping-Pong tables, canning kettles, portable closets, and wheelchairs all have fairly standard values in an estate sale, considerably below new market prices. For good antiques, however, prices may vary with the condition and rarity of the artifact and the quality of the sale in general. A good address in a stylish neighborhood, with many antiques, will produce higher asking prices than similar merchandise in a lesser sale in a bad part of town because it will bring a more knowledgeable crowd.

Since no pricer can know everything well, better-quality antiquities often require the expertise of an outside appraiser who may come in to evaluate just the oriental rugs, the paintings, or the silver. Estates which contain such specialized items as the tools of a watch repairer or ham radio operator also require knowledgeable advisors in these areas. Most estate sale professionals have a list of experts they can regularly call upon for such services. These specialists, who usually charge a flat fee, will make calls to their own regular customers and inform them of the availability of these items in the sale; occasionally they may also get a finder's fee if their customer is successful in buying the item at the time of the sale. Some outside pricers will deliberately give low evaluations to items they are interested in, and will have a stooge waiting first in line the day of the sale to snatch them up cheaply. Estate sale conductors know and trust their outside appraisers.

Once priced, the costs of items in an estate sale are firm until new rules are made, generally the second (and last) day of the sale when reductions are established. It is always problematic to leave any items unpriced. Even if done inadvertently, these overlooked items are invariably the ones picked up by the first customers in the door. Establishing a price at the cashier's, once the item has been identified by the customer who thinks a bargain is in hand, is a process which the buyer will always view with a certain degree of suspicion. It is particularly important that the cashier be someone who knows the merchandise and its prices well. The switching of price tags by would-be customers is not unknown in estate sales, where the heat of battle distracts the frenzied staff, and the preoccupation of other customers with their own hunting acts as no defense from competing shoppers who may be dishonest.

Most estate sales run two days, often Saturday and Sunday, and occasionally Friday; this ensures the largest audience as collectors have the most free time. The public is informed through ads listed under "estate sales," "house sales," or "household goods" sections of the local newspaper. While some professional firms prefer a three- or four-line ad simply stating when and where the sale is to be held, most conductors prefer a fairly lengthy ad describing the important pieces and categories of goods offered to the public. After listing furniture, rugs, major collectibles, large appliances, and other big-ticket items, the ad will frequently conclude with "many more items too numerous to mention." This inspires and assures the scrounger that items not listed can be found in quantity, and probably just the ones they are looking for.

The Public Sale

A considerable amount of adrenaline is generated by the hours of anxiety just prior to the sale, on the part of the buyers waiting with boxes in hand to gather up bargains, or by the professional staff wondering if everything is priced and if those prices are correct. The antici-

Estate sales attract collectors because of the promise of an entire intact household of goods. Eager "salers" line up early to be in the first wave to enter the house. Standing in line for an estate sale, Minneapolis. (Courtesy of Lyndly F. Opitz and Associates, Inc.)

pation of archaeologists Howard Carter and Lord Carnarvon could hardly have been more acute as they waited for the first view of King Tutankhamen's tomb than that of estate sale regulars who view each new sale with hope in their breasts as though it were an excavation of buried treasure. As a crowd-control measure, most conductors of estate sales will limit the number of persons in the house at any one time. This contributes to the security and safety of their client's property as well as providing good visibility of the merchandise and a relatively comfortable setting for the buyer. A certain amount of crowding is generally considered desirable and is thought to enhance sales as the frenzy of competition (similar to that in an auction) leads collectors to make hasty decisions.

Some dealers, hours before the sale, will pass out numbers to those waiting in line. This means that some customers may show up for

Objects formerly owned by other collectors "smell right" to the estate sale visitor. In this setting, the decision to buy an antique or collectible is often done quickly with little preparation. Dining room display of silver, glass, and porcelain at an estate sale, Minneapolis. (Courtesy of Lyndly F. Opitz and Associates, Inc.)

a 10:00 sale at 7:00, pick up a number as they would at a bakery, and be assured of their early place at the door when the sale opens. Meanwhile they can go for breakfast or sit in their warm car. Small camping vehicles, sleeping bags, lawn chairs, and thermoses of coffee are not unknown props for the competitive buyer anxious for a few comfortable hours of waiting, or for that envied position in the first wave that enters the house. The dispensing of numbers at the door of an estate sale is not without its occasional problems which vex all participants. Like ticket scalpers at a Rose Bowl game, some entrepreneurs will arrive at 5:00 a.m., get number one, and then sell it to the latecomer who doesn't mind a $20 price tag for not standing in line. Antique dealers who regularly buy at estate sales often hire someone to do this in advance. Counterfeit numbers are also produced occasionally and the hapless sale conductor is called in to be the referee.

In the mythology of antique collecting, it is often believed that the first body of customers who enter the estate sale will get the best buys. This is true certainly for those items which are fairly priced and are desirable. It is also true for grand and rare antiques whose prices, while as high as those expected in a shop, are so desirable to specialized collectors that they are anxious to have them at almost any cost. For example, two competing rug dealers, number one and number two at the door, might enter the sale abreast and simultaneously say to a sales person, "I'll take this," seemingly without inspecting it or even checking the price tag. On the other hand, later entrants into the house, particularly those who come at the end of the first day of the sale, might have the best opportunity to strike a bargain with the sale conductor.

By the end of the first day of a two-day estate sale, the conductor has usually sold what will generate far better than 50% of the expected gross. But it is not always the best merchandise—or even the bulk of it—which has sold. In fact, the first customers to the cash register may well be carrying nothing more spectacular than a lawn mower, a stack of paperbacks, or a bottle of fabric softener. Antique dealers and others who run estate sales are anxious to get top dollar for their client (and consequently for themselves) for the better items in a household, and as a result will put a good price on the best merchandise. Sometimes these prices scare off early bargain hunters and remain unsold at the end of the day. Minutes before closing on the first day is the earliest appropriate time to strike a bargain with the conductor, whose prices until then are firm. Since prices on the second day are generally reduced, this last-minute negotiation on the first day is advantageous to the buyers who may not find the desired item there if they wait to return the next day. The conductor will want as much merchandise gone from the house as possible to give a successful look to the sale when it opens the second day; thus bargaining at this point should be welcomed. Since the first strong interest expressed for an item may also be the last, it is well for the seller to consider a reasonable offer at this stage of the sale should the opportunity present itself.

Whether buying old or new merchandise, no customer wants to make purchases in a setting which looks picked over. To avoid this appearance, the staff will keep condensing the merchandise throughout the sale, and as major items are sold, rooms are cleared out and closed off. The contents of tables are condensed and neatly rearranged. With less territory to survey, the sales staff can be reduced, thus saving hourly wages. The only setting which discourages business faster than a sparsely arranged house is one too populated with underworked clerks hanging about the house like vultures with their sales books, desperately waiting for customers.

On the second day of the sale, prices are usually reduced to increase the chances of cleaning out the household. While the percentage of reduction may vary from one sale to another, it will often be something like 50% off on items under $25, and 25% off on items over that amount. Obviously, as the sale progresses to its conclusion, these percentages are more likely to become negotiable, sometimes quite dramatically. The fear by the conductor of getting stuck with items like bedroom and dining sets, sofas, pianos, organs, and other bulky goods will often prompt the vendor to make outrageous offers to any customer who looks mildly interested.

Leaving Bids

Most estate sales provide the opportunity for the customer to leave a written bid for merchandise which they wish to purchase at a reduced price. The bid slips can be completed at any time during the sale. Second-day bids, however, are best offered verbally to a sales person who is in a position to give an immediate answer. At the end of the first sale day, the conductor reviews bid slips on unsold merchandise and calls the interested parties who have left the highest bids. These bids may be only 60% of the original asking price, but nevertheless acceptable to the seller. Since hundreds of customers have already seen the item in question, including antique dealers, second-hand dealers, and junkers, and no one has been willing to pay the tag price, it probably indicates to any but the most stubborn of sellers that the tendered offer is indeed the fair market value of the item. In the case of tie bids, the earliest bid, or the first bidder who is contacted by phone, wins.

The Cleanup

There are few estate sales in which the entire contents of the household are completely sold out, down to the last boxes of canning jars, rusty-spring daybeds, and even a few collectibles. Since the conductor of the sale has contracted to leave a clean house for the client, and two days of selling have not found a buyer for every item, even at reduced price, there is still a need to get rid of the residue. This is accomplished in one of several ways.

The conductor who is also the owner of an antique shop may skim off any decent remaining merchandise at a substantially reduced cost and let it sit in the shop until it sells. If higher-priced items remain unsold, that same dealer may take them on consignment, again waiting for a customer willing to pay a good price for it. In this case the owner also waits for money due, and may not be interested in a delay in settling the estate.

Some professional conductors without shops will retain leftover merchandise and plant it into another sale later on. This is never a wise procedure, unless the material is of the kind likely to be found in almost any household. Very individual items and those identified with an earlier sale are easily spotted by regular estate-sale goers, who have memories like steel traps and are generally perturbed by antics which create stale sales of leftover household goods which they have seen before.

Most professionals faced with the task of cleaning out a house will call in a "clean-up man" who will take the good with the bad and give the conductor a set price for the remains. Clean-up people are at the lowest level of the evolutionary scale of the bizarre cast of characters selling antiques and used merchandise. They are those hapless souls who, like gleaners in the field, by virtue of their position, are forced to be content with the chaff, the leftovers which constitute the worst merchandise in the trade. They typically come into a picked-over sale, cast a disgruntled eye, complain that there is nothing of consequence left, complain about the work of handling it all, and offer a hundred or two for everything. Just as often they may offer nothing and generously agree to take away the residue without charge. The experienced conductor knows that, in order to encourage the cleaners to take on the assignment and get anything in return, a few items of some quality must be left to sweeten the bait—a wicker chair, a cute telephone stand, or a few pieces of not-so-chipped cut glass. A good clean-up man, or even a willing one, is worth knowing.

Settling the Accounts

When the sale is over and the house is empty, the conductor settles the accounts. The staff members are then paid, often in cash, though sometimes in remaining merchandise. For bookkeeping simplicity, these staff members are considered "independent agents," responsible for their own Social Security and tax records. Sales receipts, written out for each item, are totalled to determine the gross intake. The sales slips may or may not be given to the client along with their check representing all gross receipts minus the percentage charged by the conductor. The disadvantage of having the client informed of the sum of each sale means that there is room for argument and complaint if they are disappointed in what their things brought. The estate sale client is most happy for a fat check with only a vague notion of what everything brought. Rarely will estate sale conductors do a complete inventory of all objects in the house and give it to the client with the actual prices at which those items were sold. Neither the contents of the average house sale nor the inefficiency of this method would justify this as a regular practice.

Garage Sales, Yard Sales, Tag Sales

> It was the day of her yard sale and everything
> she did not care to keep was being carried into
> the yard. . . . An assortment of dinette tables and
> chairs were scattered all over the front lawn.
> There were boxes and boxes of fruit jars,
> flashlights and radios that did not work, dozens
> of mixing bowls in all colors, cups and saucers
> from Oatmeal boxes, casserole dishes,
> gooseneck lamps and miniature spoons from
> every state in the union accompanied by
> ashtrays from their capital cities. There were
> nine plastic wastepaper baskets, one with an oil
> painting of flamingos . . . and twelve T.V. trays
> with foldup legs that would surely be purchased
> the first thing . . . .
>
> Edward Swift
> *Splendora*

The most familiar and numerous of the transient sales, run by amateurs, are known in various parts of the country as garage, yard, or tag sales. In the last decade, the family-run sale of household miscellany has increased to startling proportions. It is not unusual for local newspaper ads to feature through the better part of the year several pages listing such sales, by neighborhood, throughout the city. In some municipalities, it has become such big business that its operation is regulated by laws which require the purchase of a temporary license to do business, and limits are placed on the number of sales per year which any individual may hold. The increased sensitivity of nearly everyone in recent years to the cash value of their unwanted goods, and their own willingness to sell it directly, has seriously affected the flow of better merchandise into the charity agencies who run second-hand shops nationwide. *Charity shops* these days are filled almost entirely with used clothing and pots and pans, books, and broken household electrics. In the 1950s and '60s such retail establishments still showed good furniture of the Victorian and golden-oak periods. One would be lucky these days to find a high-style chrome dinette set.

Garage sales offer a full range of household goods, furniture, appliances, and knickknacks, but probably more chance of finding collectibles than important antiques. Suburban garage sale. (Courtesy of Minneapolis Star and Tribune)

A successful family-run sale is accomplished with the same kind, though not the same degree, of planning and organization which a larger estate sale requires. In order to be worth doing at all, the items included for sale must be worth buying. If a family is ridding itself of a burned-out toaster or a broken stereo, it is unlikely that any other family will want it either. Buyers at garage sales, regardless of how poor they may be, nevertheless want things which are clean, complete, and working. Normal wear and tear is expected, but one ski pole, a cut-glass sugar bowl with a large crack, or a stained and rotted 1890s wedding dress is of little value to anyone.

In recent years the multi-family sale has become popular. Sometimes these are called *block sales* and the entire neighborhood participates, each neighbor being responsible for marking and selling his or her own property. The advantage to this system is that there is much more merchandise, and of greater variety, to attract customers. The costs and labor of promotion in local papers and neighborhood signage (if it is permitted by local ordinance) may be equitably shared. There are essentially three rules for running a garage, yard, or tag sale: (1) everything for sale should be useful to someone and should be clean, (2) everything should be priced, and (3) the price should be negotiable. Fair prices at these sales should *start* at ⅓ to ½ of what was originally paid for it.

For the serious collector of antiques, family-run sales are probably not worth the time they take to survey. Driving from one end of town to the other, getting in and out of a car twenty or thirty times, plus the cost of the gas and patience to do it, may be more investment than all but the most eager *salers* will want to make. Collectibles enthusiasts, however, will probably spend the majority of their time at such sales as well as at flea markets rather than in established shops. Families having children leaving home, who go into retirement, or do their spring cleaning are likely to bring baseball cards, old comics, used sports equipment, old tools, wedding gifts, and home furnishings from the '50s into the open. The growing interest in ephemera—relatively recent cultural material not classifiable as antique—as well as in the "fabulous '40s and '50s" has given the garage sale, yard sale, or tag sale an enthusiastic new clientele.

5

The People in the Business

Dealing with Dealers

> We dealers are pretty slick. Some are all right,
> but some are not. We're good and bad, mixed.
> There are grafters, crooks, conners, lifters,
> zangers, edgers, pullers, professional dummyers,
> clippers—every variety of bloke on the
> make. . . . Cleverer than any artists, better than
> any actor.
>
> Jonathan Gash
> *The Judas Pair*

Just because the buying of antiques is highly competitive and requires wit, nerve, and cunning does not mean that it is without its rules. Nor does it mean that neither morality nor etiquette is connected with its practices. Those who are most familiar with the broader antique market realize that it is nevertheless a small world filled with people who gossip and who know each other and each other's inventories. It is only prudent, then, for a collector to participate as little as possible in loose talk, and, in general, to respect the people with whom one is dealing. In a big department store, clerks may not care at all about what customers say regarding the merchandise, since the former have no personal stake in its quality, price, or selection; they may, in fact, sympathize with the customer who finds that nothing fits, everything is too expensive, and things are made poorly. The average antique dealers, however, are different; they not only clerk in their shops but own them. Additionally, they have a very personal interest in what the customer thinks and says about their merchandise, since the assembled goods represent a combination of their taste, intelligence, and choice. The very act of walking into an antique shop means that the customer has entered the private space of the vendor, and should act as thoughtfully as if in someone's home. A simple, friendly "Hello" to the dealer should be enough to start out on the right foot. Customers perceived by the dealer to be thoughtless are not likely to be given the time of day let alone any deferential treatment when it comes time for price negotiations or any other special acts of assistance. Thus, the customer does well to remember some general rules of etiquette.

Many antique shops are small and most are crowded with break-ables of all sorts, so it is to everyone's advantage to protect the goods from damage. Bulky coats, dangling purses, and swinging umbrellas are the biggest dangers to merchandise with the exception of small children and large dogs. Dealers will be happy to hold customers' packages behind the counter or store their wraps while they shop in comfort. An enthusiastic overreaching for a pretty vase on a high shelf, or for a fragile figurine across a deep counter, is commonly done in the heat of the hunt for antiques, and can easily lead to disaster.

The ubiquitous "You Break It, You Bought It" signs in antique shops should be ample reminders of the embarrassment caused to both parties when accidents do occur. Having to pay for something which one has just damaged or destroyed, and probably didn't want at all, is very painful indeed. On the unhappy chance that a customer does inadvertently cause damage, it is not uncommon that the dealer will be gracious enough to reduce the tag price on the broken item and ask for compensation only to cover the cost of investment. No one in this situation, however, ought to *expect* such an act of mercy, and should be prepared to pay the full marked price. Sensible dealers, of course, do not display negative and threatening signs about breakage, but rather prevent accidents by anticipating them, making certain that especially breakable items are put in appropriate cases and inventory is displayed in such a way that it cannot be kicked, bumped, or tripped over. Neither smoking nor eating by customers in antique shops is appropri-ate even if the dealer is so engaged. If dealers damage their own mer-chandise by the carelessness associated with these acts, it is far better than the customer doing so.

Antique dealers who are sensitive to their customers are aware that pleasant conversation often increases buyer interest, frequently fol-lowed by a purchase. Productive dialogue with dealers can provide the interested customer with considerable information about antiques, and the best dealers are eager to tell what they know to customers who show enthusiasm for learning. Dealers are aware that uninformed and ignorant people are not likely to buy anything, and that the customers who spend the most on antiques are the ones who know the most about them. It is, in part, the job of the vendor to provide opportunities for this kind of informal instruction so likely to take place between seller and buyer; it is simply good business.

Serious collectors never go in *groups* when they are looking for antiques. The rush into a shop of four or five friends, killing a few hours by bumming for collectibles, is not likely to engender much sympathy from dealers who must act as host or hostess to such cattle. These are often the same people who would happily pay $5 or $10 to see merchandise at an overpriced antique show, but come to a shop and see similar goods for free, complain about the prices, and expect the same degree of entertainment. Dealers realize that most visitors are "just looking," but customers who ask specifically for certain items which the dealer might be helpful in locating for them are likely to be regarded more seriously when they appear to be knowledgeable about some area of collecting.

Conversation between dealers and customers, unless they know each other very well, is best limited to topics of mutual interest related to antiques. Even within this arena, there are discussions best left unsaid. Talking about other dealers and what they have is of little interest, and possibly a source of irritation, to dealers trying to sell their own wares. No dealer is interested in what some prospective customer just bought in the shop next door, or in all the fabulous things they have at home that they bought for next to nothing. Neither are dealers interested in what anyone's grandmother had or in conversation which includes descriptions of their own family heirlooms such as, "We had one just like this, except ours was better," or, "We threw ours out years ago; never thought it was worth this much." There are plenty of antique collectors who think it is fair game to walk into a shop and proceed to downgrade the premises, the merchandise, the prices, the dirt, the smell, or the disarray. Yielding to this temptation is best done privately and away from the shop, other customers, and dealers.

Discussing the objects one encounters in a shop, and even their prices, is a perfectly appropriate thing to do. Seeing remarkable, interesting, and even familiar antiques quite naturally generates comment among customers and with the dealer. However, a certain discretion should be exercised in guiding the conversation. For example, visitors to antique shops should never seem shocked by prices. If they express their horror at high price tags, they are conveying the message to the vendor that they are unsophisticated, unappreciative, or just plain cheap. If a customer says, "I just saw one identical to this in a shop last week, and it was only half this price," it might just be that the dealer *bought* it from that shop last week, thinking a profit could be made from it in his own establishment. Prices of antiques, in any case, are based upon what the dealer paid for them, and two identical items for which differing amounts were paid may rightly bear different price tags.

Without thinking how their query sounds, some customers will boldly ask a dealer, "Where did you get this?" upon finding a remarkable item in his or her shop. Despite the innocence of the question, and the fact that the customer is probably only making an observation on the rarity of the object, it sounds to the dealer either like an accusation that the item was gotten illegally, or that they are being asked to reveal their source of inventory. Customers whose curiosity is so keen might better phrase the question in some less accusatory manner: "I'm surprised you can even *find* such a wonderful item; did you get it locally?"

Unlike ordinary retail stores where prices are fixed by unseen management, the prices found in antique stores are determined by the buyer who is also the seller. Because of the direct contact between the customer and the dealer, antique buyers regularly assume that prices are negotiable, and most dealers expect that they will be asked for discounts. A seasoned shopper eventually knows which shops and which dealers have *firm* prices from which they will not waver. Some such shops display the familiar though unfriendly sign:

> I found it, hauled it, cleaned it, repaired it,
> researched it, priced it, paid the rent, insurance
> and advertising, and YOU want me to take LESS
> for it?

Shops like this, fortunately, are in the minority, and most dealers are not offended by being asked about price. Regularly dealers give discounts of 10% or more to other dealers as a professional courtesy, and usually they will give as much to any other interested buyer, particularly on days when the rent is due.

How dealers are asked makes a big difference in the way they respond to questions about pricing. A customer should never *offer* a dealer a price such as, "I'll give you $85 for it." Rather, it is the prerogative of the dealer to set the price, which is then agreed to or not by the customer. There are perfectly acceptable ways to ask that a lower price be considered. The flaws in merchandise or their high prices should be of absolutely no concern to the customer unless they are interested in buying the piece. Pointing out every chip, crack, or missing part is not the way to make a dealer lower a price. If a piece is flawed enough to warrant a lower price, no respectable collector should want it anyway. The least offensive ways of asking for a price reduction include such phrases as, "Are your prices firm?" "Can you do better on this?" or "Is this your lowest price?" Almost always a dealer will make some concession to the customer, enough, at least, to compensate for the sales tax. If not, the dealer may even explain that he or she cannot lower the price, since "That's almost what I have in it."

Occasionally, and sometimes frequently, customers know more than dealers about the goods they are selling. No matter how helpful it may seem at the time, it is unwise to let them know that their prices are foolishly low or high, or that their attributions of age, authorship, or authenticity are faulty. Again, unless these complaints are specifically related to items being purchased, they are of no concern to the customer. In any event, most dealers are not likely to thank a customer for pointing out flaws in their merchandise or errors in their judgment. Leaving an antique store, like entering one, is an appropriate time for some pleasant remark. Even if the customer has made a purchase, though especially if not, the proprietor should be thanked for time and attention taken. A positive remark or two about the shop is always appreciated, even if it can be nothing more flattering than praising the ample parking.

Pickers, Runners, and Divvies

> Scouts? We call them barkers, in the trade. An
> antique dealer has scouts, people who will pass
> information his way. Tinker Dill was one of
> mine. I have three of four, depending on how
> rich I'm feeling at the time, paid on commission.
>
> Jonathan Gash
> *The Judas Pair*

A picker is a dealer in antiques who acts as an independent buying and selling agent to a loosely defined group of customers, most of whom are other dealers. Since they seldom deal directly with the public, pickers are largely invisible to most collectors. A picker does not have a shop, and usually has no inventory other than what he or she has found in the last few days. It is the picker's self-appointed job to know what every dealer has and wants, to be everywhere at once, and make the transactions quickly to the profit of all parties. The work which pickers perform can best be described as the wholesaling of antiques. In England, those who do the job of picking are appropriately referred to as *runners* and *divvies*. Runners also act independently by running artifacts from one dealer to another with a relatively small markup in the bargain. Divvies (from the word "divine," meaning to discover intuitively) work on commission or by-the-job payment and are often attached to one or several dealers specifically seeking out requested items or even just information about the location of desired antiquities.

Like antique dealers, some pickers work full time and others do it as a supplement to a primary income. Since their enterprise has no permanent location (other than that indicated by their home phone number), no easily identifiable business expenses or provable profits (their transactions are often in cash), many pickers operate just outside the parameters of legitimate business and not infrequently avoid the constraints of licenses, sales, and income tax. Antique dealers who regularly bear considerable overhead, and who take their business and civic responsibilities seriously, often have a natural antipathy for pickers who appear, in many ways, to have the best of both worlds; they have a high-activity level of trading, and no burdens of rent, insurance, and regular hours. But like the birds who live on the backs of hippopotami eating pesky insects, the relationship of dealer and picker is a symbiotic one.

The average picker, if there is such a person, is an "action junkie" whose need for constant antique dealing probably exceeds that of the most avid private collectors. Pickers are intimately familiar with the contents of antique shops which they visit with regularity. They also know what kind of merchandise any given proprietor prefers to deal in and what they are willing to pay for it. While they will occasionally have specific orders to find particular antiques for dealers, most pickers buy what they can cheaply, and then seek the right customers for them. Watching a picker in action is like seeing a rat in a maze. They nervously nose about in likely and unlikely places—auctions, flea markets, garage and estate sales—as well as buying directly from private owners. Sometimes they are the foot-in-the-door characters who prowl ordinary neighborhoods to knock on doors and ask the inhabitants if they have any antiques, giving the trusting owners pennies on the dollar of their actual worth. They live, talk, and dream antiques, and their favorite topic of conversation seldom drifts even to the weather.

Since pickers are wholesalers, they must buy at a below whole-sale cost, especially if they are selling to dealers who, in turn, must also make a profit. If they sell to private collectors they will charge more. This is the area of antiquing that allows for the least margin of error, and the keenest sense for the realistic assessment of market prices. Pickers look for *sleepers*, for merchandise of quality which is underpriced in shops or elsewhere. Their profit markup may vary with each transaction, but it is often below the usual 100% expected by the shop dealers. The skill of being a picker requires a talent for the rapid turnover of merchandise, very often the same day it is purchased. For this reason, the picker who has just bought a silver service, oriental rug, or a notable painting may be willing to immediately sell to a dealer at a quick 25% commission. Naturally the picker will try to extract as much as possible, but is always guided by the knowledge that those to whom he sells must also profit from its resale. The private world of trading inhabited by the picker is based on an eye for quality and the previously unnoticed, upon volume dealing, and upon holding no antique a minute longer than necessary.

Who Are the Experts?

> The phrase "consult an expert" leads nowhere.
> Where *is* the expert? If he is a dealer, he is
> selling his own goods. If he is *not* a dealer the
> question is embarrassing, because, unless he
> takes time to make certain regarding the
> antiquity of the piece, he is likely to be running
> into serious trouble for the future. There is no
> professional appraiser of antique furniture,
> though some persons act in that capacity on
> occasion.
>
> Wallace Nutting
> *Furniture Treasury*

Many amateurs, and some even more experienced in antique collecting, hold the notion that somewhere there are people who are the final authorities on antiques; they are the ones who know everything; they are the leading authorities; they are the experts. One needs to understand relatively little about science, law, or the military to realize that so-called experts in those fields are challenged daily regarding their relative knowledge of their respective disciplines. Even more so in the areas of art and antiques, where criteria of quality and authenticity are more often a matter of argument, it is especially difficult to assign the title of *expert*.

The question of who then *are* the experts is one which is open to considerable discussion. Wallace Nutting, while himself considered by many to be the most authoritative figure in the field of early American furniture, even decades after his death, held a very definite opinion on the subject and strongly denied that such a thing as an expert actually existed.

The expert is often the person who happens to be correct at the time asked for an opinion. An expert might be the representative for an auction house whose estimates are realized at sale, or the New York City antique dealer who senses that a highboy is fake, or the museum curator who buys an important Etruscan bronze with someone else's money, or the art historian with a Ph.D. who "discovers" an artist, then makes him famous. When the sale price at auction more than doubles its estimate, however, when the dealer ignores intuition and buys a dud, when new scholarship casts doubt on a museum purchase, or when another art historian pans a recent monograph, then the "experts" responsible for decisions which initially made them glow with brilliance are no longer authorities in the minds of the public. Experts, it is probably safe to say, are those who appear to be correct in their judgments much more frequently than they are wrong.

The field of antiques is, in one sense, no different than that of law or religion. Any established standards or rules (of which there are many) are open to interpretation, and any agreement by two experts in the value of a single antique is what makes prices soar at auction, an inflation which halts only when one opinion deems the price too high. No matter how knowledgeable, no one is *always* correct in judgment, nor do similarly qualified experts necessarily always agree. A case in point is the Rembrandt Commission, established in 1969 to celebrate the tricentenary of the painter's death. Its purpose was to examine and review all known paintings of Rembrandt and compile a report of the findings. The panel charged with this awesome task, of which establishing authenticity of the pictures was a primary goal, consisted of the most distinguished scholars in the field of seventeenth-century Netherlandish art. For many pictures, after personal examination of the art, there was general consensus that they were genuine; on others there was considerable disagreement. For one picture, *Man with the Golden Helmet*, the treasured and much publicized masterpiece of the State Museum in East Berlin, there was general agreement by the experts who concluded that it was genuine. Years later, in 1984, the same picture came under considerable scrutiny, and was declared by a new generation of authorities *not* to be by Rembrandt at all. Who is actually correct on this matter still remains to be seen.

Experts in the field of antique collecting, whatever qualifications such a title might entail, are generally called upon for two different, though related, kinds of advice. Either they are expected to *authenticate* an antique by commenting on its age, authorship, and condition, or they are asked to *evaluate* it by assigning it a price. Sometimes these tasks may be done by a single person, sometimes not. Authenticators tend to be those experts outside the fields of buying and selling, who may not even quote dollar evaluations in their work. Naturally, objective individuals, who have no personal stake in the antique being judged, are the least likely to be suspect when they give their opinion regarding its quality. Evaluators are, essentially, appraisers, and are more thoroughly discussed later in the following section.

Museum personnel, because of their training and daily familiarity with objects of quality, are frequently asked to be authenticators when there are questions about items of major consequence. Museum per-

sonnel, and curators in particular, have earned an unfortunate reputation in the past for their aloofness and their general inaccessibility to the
public. In the last few years, fortunately, this has begun to change as
museums, fighting for survival in a world of few arts dollars, are willing
to do almost anything to make themselves relevant to segments of the
population less elite than the ones they formerly served. Many museums regularly hold expertise clinics in which anyone off the street
with a curious object can use the knowledge assembled there and ascertain the identity of his or her objects. Museums, by virtue of their
responsibility as educational institutions, and because of established
policy, are disallowed from quoting monetary evaluations when examining items brought in by the public.

Scholars, usually art historians or archaeologists connected with
universities, and who publish in areas such as classical sculpture, ro-
manesque bronzes, mannerist painting, or WPA murals, for example,
are another likely source for the expertise required to authenticate such
material objects that might be in question. Like curators, scholars study
museum collections as well as private collections, and have field experience of considerable depth. Scholars are also familiar with related
literature and archival sources and tend to know their own areas with
an intimacy which often borders on monomania. They are often flat-
tered when contacted about their specialty, and predictably generate
useful responses to intelligent inquiries.

The act of becoming an expert has traditionally been accomplished more through experience than by formal education. Most of
those who are considered antique experts outside museums and colleges have learned their craft through the school of hard knocks and
daily practice rather than by formal training specifically intended to
educate practitioners in the antique field. There are, in fact, relatively
few places nationally which teach the kinds of subjects that would
educate one toward becoming an antique expert per se. The distinguished course of study at Winterthur, Delaware, is a major exception.
In conjunction with the University of Delaware art history and American studies programs, it is one of the few which exclusively deals with
decorative arts and the material culture in its relationship to history. This
graduate curriculum leads to a master's degree, and produces highly
trained candidates for museum and historical-society work. Most other
museology programs throughout the United States concentrate on museum management and practice, rather than on expertise and connoisseurship of objects as stressed in the Winterthur program.

The older and larger historical installations regularly host workshops and seminars on antiquities. The New York Historical Association

in Cooperstown offers summer seminars in American Culture; Williamsburg hosts the Antiques Forum in February; and Greenfield Village in Detroit and Old Sturbridge Village in Massachusetts hold regular antique forums available to anyone who pays the tuition. Academics, however, are more likely to avail themselves of such enlightenment than are antique dealers and appraisers who might well need such information in their businesses.

Other specialists, frequently self-styled and self-taught, are those who write books and articles about collecting, many of which are superb, others not. The best of these writers assimilate enormous amounts of information on a particular subject such as collecting old photographs, Hull Pottery, Gaudy Welsh, antique doorknobs, Susie Cooper pottery, transportation postcards, railroad memorabilia, and other areas of focus. The best of these sources gives an account of the history of the production of such items and sets the specialty within the context of its time. It may outline the business aspects of the company that made the objects, naming owners, designers, artists, promoters, and dates whenever appropriate. Pattern names and dates, original costs, shape and size, inventories, and distribution procedures are all topics of interest to collectors, which are often included in such texts. Usually books of this sort are heavily illustrated with examples which may be very useful for collectors attempting to identify their own particular pieces. Occasionally these books consist largely of examples from the personal collection of the writer who may or may not have any substantive reason for its writing aside from showing off his or her own accumulation. Many collectors, unfortunately, are primarily concerned with what their own things are worth, and the inclusion of *price lists* (which are soon out of date) is often what sells the book.

Real experts on various antique subjects can also certainly be found among those regularly encountered in the buying and selling of antiques. These are the dealers, auctioneers, pickers, and other collectors who, by virtue of their handling quantities of antiques, are bound to know a great deal about a number of subject areas. Their knowledge is often not consistently even in all areas, nor very orderly in its application. Collectors and dealers are the "street-wise" characters who inhabit the world of antiques; they have learned from the experience of both failure and success and their counsel is usually worth heeding. Particularly on an informal basis, the clever listener can gain volumes of information and collecting tips from these people who generally love talking about what they know best. Gaining from the experience of others is the least painful kind of learning in a field where one's own mistakes may cost dearly.

Appraisers

> He stared at the jeweled egg resting in the palm
> of his hand. After a moment he looked at Duffy,
> then back at the egg. Ben's calculations collided
> with one another as he tried converting Miss
> Natalie's estate into something of value, jewels
> into dollars, history into net worth.
>
> Nan and Ivan Lyons
> *Sold!*

Appraisers are yet another kind of expert within the antique trade. It is the job of the appraiser to evaluate in actual dollars and cents the value of objects of art and antiques. For good reason, appraisers may be some of the most knowledgeable people in the antique field, since their evaluation of goods requires not only a familiarity with current pricing, but they must simultaneously be able to assess the inherent worth of objects by judging their authenticity, condition, and age. Those who appraise for insurance, inheritance, or tax purposes are also bound by law to provide upon request documentation for the evaluations which they have made.

Appraisers are likely to come out of a background of antique selling. Some have discovered that good money can be made just from what they know as much as from what they might sell from a shop. The best of these make their living exclusively by evaluating antiques, others do it on a part-time basis as a regular part of their shop business or in conducting estate sales. Many fewer of them have taken workshops and participated in studies programs given throughout the country. Certificate programs on appraising are offered, for example, at such places as Yeshiva University in New York, which enable appraisers to take short sessions in such subjects as appraising art and decorative arts; identifying and appraising antique and modern silver; and appraising estate jewelry, American, English and Continental furniture, collectibles, and Americana. These courses are intensive and are taught by those in the appraisal and allied fields. They are truly workshops, focusing on specifics, and are not lengthy, extensive courses with the kind of historical or analytical approach to material culture which baccalaureate or graduate degree programs in universities provide. The 6,000-member American Society of Appraisers does sponsor a degree program in Valuation Sciences offered at several colleges throughout the country.

Appraisers are obliged to keep abreast of current trends and evaluations in the antique market. In part, this is accomplished by subscribing to innumerable periodicals, including collecting magazines, price guides, trade journals, and auction catalogs. Memberships in such groups as The American Society of Appraisers, or in the smaller Appraisers Association of America, may provide the members with newsletters, trade journals, bulletins, and continuing education opportunities. The mere fact that dealers or appraisers are members of any such organization does not necessarily mean that they are experts, nor that they are any more qualified to make an accurate or honest appraisal than anyone else similarly familiar with the business.

Ironically, a full membership in the ASA requires two years of full-time experience in appraisals (presumably while not yet qualified as a professional), and the passing of a written examination, as well as an interview with the examiners. It may also require sponsorship of the candidate by an already established appraisal practitioner. Membership qualifications in the AAA, according to their own application form, are somewhat looser and are " . . . open to all qualified individuals in the antique, art and collectible field [for at least three years], on approval of the Board of Directors." These and other dealers' associations usually espouse a code of ethics which involves the maintenance of high standards and professional behavior.

Those appraisers who join such groups do it primarily for the benefit of increased public trust; the public expects professionals to belong to professional organizations. The field of appraising, however, cannot be rightly considered a profession in the way medicine, law, teaching, or even airplane mechanics are, since it does not enforce standardized educational procedures and qualifications. The actual licensing of appraisers has not yet become a reality, but it is reasonable to assume that as greater responsibility falls upon its practitioners, there is the likelihood of its becoming regulated by this method.

As with the practice of many other arts (rather than sciences), skilled appraising depends heavily upon experience. Like dealers, appraisers typically have seen, handled, and analyzed thousands upon thousands of antiques. They generally have minds which are encyclopedic in this area, and can remember an object, a price, or an entire collection with the greatest precision and detail. Their memory for visual images and prices of related objects in the market gives them the basis for comparison of the antiquities which they are called upon to appraise. Some appraisers specialize and become well known in a particular area such as silver, costumes and textiles, jewelry and watches, fine art, or period furniture. In the evaluation of a large estate, for example, various appraisers, each with their own area of expertise, may be called upon to give their opinions regarding the stamp collection, the Oceanic sculpture, the religious vestments, or the Piranesi folios.

The accurate value of an antique is usually needed for one of several reasons; it is used for insurance, tax, or resale purposes. Since the evaluation figure quoted by the appraiser in each of these cases might be different for the same object, collectors who need appraisals should make it clear from the beginning as to the *purpose* of the evaluation they seek. Usually the professional appraiser will ask (or already knows) what the intended purpose of the appraisal is, and will act accordingly. Appraisers who are evaluating a single piece or an entire collection for insurance purposes are likely to choose a high figure which reasonably reflects actual replacement cost in the current (and appreciating) market. Highest appraisals, at demonstrated market values, are also given to property of potential donors, which is being given to public institutions for the tax advantages. In both instances it is the owner of the goods who pays for the appraisal. Low market evaluations tend to be made on property which is part of an estate. Subsequent inheritors of the property from the estate desire appraisals as low as is reasonable to minimize their own tax responsibilities.

Appraising, unfortunately, is not limited exclusively to those who do it as a full-time job. Almost everyone at every level of the antique trade, at some time or another, gives appraisals. The free informal verbal appraisals given by these people are best used as general guidelines by the recipients and are, for all intents and purposes, as worthy as their cost. One seeking an appraisal should be reminded that *vendors* of antiques, while often knowledgeable about their subject, are not the most objective source for advice. For example, if a choice antique, such as a ruby, pressed-glass kerosene lamp in the Lincoln Drape pattern, is brought to a vendor for evaluation, it is unlikely that that dealer, anxious to have such a plum in stock, would give it a fair price on the chance that the owner, upon hearing any price, might sell it directly to the dealer.

In the business of appraisals, there is, apparently, no one system whereby fees are charged for the services. While some appraisers will charge a percentage of the value of the property for their fees, (somewhere around 5%), such persons are usually to be avoided for the obvious reason that they may tend to over-evaluate the objects in order to increase their own salary. More frequently, appraisers will charge a flat rate for single items, and will determine their charges for a number of items, or a whole house full, by an hourly fee. Time and knowledge are what an appraiser is selling, and travel and research time are considerable in larger jobs. It is not unusual for appraisers to charge between $50 and $100 per hour or more for their advice.

Few reliable appraisers will give an immediate on-the-spot evaluation, but will do their homework before assigning a dollar figure to the client's property. Finding comparable items in auction catalogs and other sources is essential to establish legitimate values. Each appraised item is listed separately, described in enough detail to be accurate and useful for the insurance company, bank, or Internal Revenue Service using the information. In the listing, style, age, material, maker, condition, size, and color are usually described, along with an assigned dollar amount included for each item.

6

THE PRICING OF ANTIQUES

It is strange to think that this precious British
Guiana one-cent magenta once belonged to me.
Sixty-one years ago I unearthed it and sold it for
six shillings, Now it is shown in a glass case all
by itself when on exhibition, with a bodyguard
of detectives to look after it.

L. Vernon Vaughan, in a letter to the
London *Daily Mail*, 1934

Assessing the value of an antique and pricing it appropriately is probably the most mysterious aspect of the entire business to both vendor and buyer. In one sense, antiques are no different than any other goods which are sold; they are worth whatever anyone is willing to pay for them. Like new goods, the circumstance of their sale is directly related to their cost, and like things which are new, they can be bought wholesale or retail, or at any of the stages in between. Antiques may be purchased from those desperate for cash, from those indifferent to a sale, or even from people reluctant to part with their property. Sellers of antiques may be completely ignorant of their value, or may be extremely knowledgeable as to their intrinsic or monetary worth; all these factors have a direct bearing on what they will charge for them. No antique has an absolute *right* price. Even the authors of the numerous useful price guides which fill the market are the first to admit that the prices which they quote in their books are meant to be a general guide to dealers so they will not "give anything away" and to collectors so they will not "get stung" on overpriced merchandise.

The *price* of an antique and its *value* are really two different, though related, topics for the knowledgeable buyer to consider. Value in an antique is established by the qualities inherent in the object itself, or in its history. These may be a combination of any of the following factors: rarity, condition, beauty, historical importance, or even who owned it. Value, which is a much more elusive quality, is determined by the overall integrity of the object in relationship to its environment. The price of an antique, of course, is also based upon all those factors which affect its value, but also equally upon the external conditions of its sale such as time, place, and economy. The same Tiffany lamp, for instance, sold new in 1902 might have cost the buyer $250, whereas in 1940 when it was hopelessly out of fashion it might have brought $50, and in 1960 the lucky owner may have sold it for $1,800. Today the same lamp could easily realize a retail price of $2,800. Which price was the correct one? The answer, of course, is that they *all* were. The *time* (date) when an antique is sold, which also corresponds to its relative popularity, quite naturally affects its selling price. The *place* where an antique is sold—an auction, estate sale, specialty shop—as well as the geography—Birmingham, Duluth, Houston, New York, San Francisco—are factors which cannot be overlooked in discussing the price of antiques.

What the vendor paid for the antique is a critical consideration in its pricing. Three identical objects found in three different shops in the same city might easily have three different prices. This is simply because the dealers who have them probably paid three different prices for them, and their asking price reflects the doubling of those figures. The following section will detail those features which influence the value and price of an antique.

What Affects the Price of an Antique?
Design

Design is the overwhelmingly important factor in determining the value of an antique. It is design quality which has made what are now antiques desirable in any period, and it is what distinguishes them from the vast quantities of ordinary goods produced in any age. Whether one follows the New York auction prices or the pricing of dealers who work the local flea markets, the relative superiority of an object's appearance strongly affects its desirability in the market, and therefore its price. The preeminence of design as a decisive element in determining an antique's value can be easily illustrated.

Two eighteenth-century chests of drawers, for example, might have been made in the same period, the same city, even the same workshop; they may be of the same wood, the same size, in the same state of preservation, and have come from the same original owner, yet their market prices may differ dramatically. The disparity in their prices is due neither to age, provenance, nor physical condition; it relies rather on the specific features of their respective designs. A further comparison of the two pieces in question may show that the better piece has a nicely shaped apron more integral to its overall design; the brasses may be more carefully selected and placed; the drawers are graduated in size, not identical; the drawer fronts are slightly bowed rather than straight and their grain is perfectly matched to create a rhythmic pattern.

Major antique houses who offer furniture of quality to the public regularly describe the subtlety of design features as the focus of their advertisements. The wording of such ads is often as skillful as the execution of the objects themselves. Several Chippendale pieces have been described in the following way: "The execution of the piecrust edge of the single board top, squashed ball, and acanthus carved legs are exceptional," "The boldly conceived and skillfully executed cyma-scalloped marble top has a generous overhang and finely molded edge,"

A dated Scandinavian box might lure the collector because of its date. The 1891 example, however, is a factory-made tourist piece, but the other is a genuine hand-wrought immigrant tine. Norwegian factory-made covered box (dated 1891). Goldstein Gallery, gift of Leona A. Schwab in memory of Prof. and Mrs. Elvin Stakman. Mid-nineteenth-century Swedish immigrant tine. Hennepin County Historical Society, Minneapolis. (Photo: Jim Barbour)

The alteration of a Georgian pewter mug into a pitcher in
the late nineteenth century by the addition of a spout
makes it more useful but less valuable. English mid-
Georgian pewter mug. Goldstein Gallery, gift of Charlotte
and Ralph Jacobsen. (Photo: Judy Olausen, courtesy of
Goldstein Gallery)

and "Orderly perfection . . . the piece displays a superior sense of design with its bonnet top cresting the case." The narrative accompanying a pilgrim piece may draw attention to a single exceptional detail of design such as "superlative vase and ring turnings."

In an additional comparison of two other objects, design quality is still fundamental to their worth. Two early Rookwood vases, for example (both made in 1894, turned by the same potter, and decorated by the same artist), could each realize a different price in an auction or in a shop. Once again, a comparison of design elements is critical in determining both value and cost. In any piece of decorated ceramics, it is the perfection of the shape and its relationship to the decoration which insures its success as a unified design. One pot, for example, might have a stiffly painted single blossom placed uncomfortably on an unflattering background, whereas another vase might reveal sensitively articulated floral forms which seem to grow from the field on which they are painted; they wrap graciously around the vessel and become an integral part of its overall artistic statement. Two "flow-blue" decorated transferware Staffordshire platters from the same factory will be priced according to their quality if one has a generic English landscape on it and the other depicts the more interesting narrative scene of the *Landing of Lafayette*.

In the design analysis of antiques, the principle of proportion cannot be overemphasized; this is perhaps particularly true in the case of furniture. Essentially a mathematical concept, proportion considers the relationship of parts to other parts, and the relationship of parts to the whole. Proportion also has to do with the size of a piece in relation to its surroundings. Any auctioneer or dealer knows that a small, sensitively scaled sideboard or rocking chair will sell better than one which is oversized and clunky. While nevertheless magnificent, the sheer bulk of a nine-foot-high Renaissance revival Victorian bed may limit the number of potential owners because its size alone precludes its utility in many smaller living quarters. Again, it is the sophisticated dealers who call attention to this quality in their advertisements. Such ads which reveal a sensitivity to proportion may read as follows: " . . . sophisticated clock . . . the graceful proportions set off by figured crossbanding," " . . . well-proportioned drawers," or "A fine small Baltimore sideboard with delicate fan inlay." Good proportion is one feature of antiquities which is either present or not; it is integral and cannot be "added on." All the details of embellishment, fineness of finish, or the persuasiveness of verbal or written records regarding its provenance cannot compensate for what is an initially clumsy piece.

In any antique, the sum of the parts is always greater than any individual component no matter how magnificently wrought each may

One Rookwood vase, produced nine years later than the other, is nevertheless more than twice as valuable because it is a unique hand-turned and decorated piece rather than simply cast in a mold. Hand-turned and painted Rookwood vase, Cincinnati, Ohio, decorated by Sara Elizabeth Coyne, 1925. Goldstein Gallery, Harriet and Vetta Goldstein Estate purchase. Cast Rookwood vase, Cincinnati, Ohio, 1916. Goldstein Gallery, Kinsley H. Murphy Estate. (Photo: Jim Barbour)

be. It is ultimately the *beauty* and *style* of a piece, in both its particulars and in its whole, which give an antique its identity and provide its owners with lasting pleasure.

The *style* of a piece of glass or furniture, carpet, stained glass window, or piece of silver plate is, essentially, its outward appearance. Style is composed of individual elements in a vocabulary of design motifs and features which give any designed object its character. It is style which ultimately sets objects apart from one another and gives them the identity of their respective historical periods, their geographical origins, or even their makers. The combined unity of separate, describable features makes something look Gothic, baroque, rococo, or Art Deco.

It is style which makes twenty-year-old cars, five-year-old computers, or last year's dresses seem outdated. Art Nouveau and Mission (arts and crafts) are easily distinguished from one another because of their contrasting styles. Their respective uses of design elements of line, form, and color are as dramatically different as is their adherence to various interpretations of the design principles of balance, proportion, emphasis, and rhythm. Attention to style and other design features in the manufacture of an object of any age is what makes it "look right" to observers. It is the familiarity with what genuine, period antiques should look like which allows an experienced collector to declare upon examining an item in question that it does or does not "feel right." Seeing twenty pieces of eighteenth-century Wedgwood in a museum should give someone who spots the twenty-first piece in a garage sale some notion of whether or not it too is correct. While style happens deliberately, it also happens inadvertently.

A "Chippendale" highboy made in the Victorian period, no matter how carefully it was copied from the eighteenth-century original, almost always has a look about it which betrays its true identity as a reproduction because of subtle changes which the copier makes unknowingly. The technically accomplished, though deliberately faked, paintings in the style of Johannes Vermeer (1632–1675), so cleverly done by Han van Meegeren (1889–1947) before the Second World War fooled many experts including historians, museum personnel, and private collectors. To more recent eyes, however, his "seventeenth-century" portraits have a rather twentieth-century look that went unnoticed by those living closer to the period in which the deception was accomplished. No age, it seems, can fail to impart something of its own taste and character onto the past which it admires.

Developing a sensitivity to design quality and style in antiques is a skill which happens so slowly and subtly than many are willing to call it an innate talent or intuition, or believe it to be something quite magical. Curiously, after a lifetime of handling objects, some dealers and collectors are no more equipped with this attribute than are some beginners. Nevertheless, it is a quality that is essential to being good in the trade—in either a buying or selling capacity. But it is a skill also achievable through a combined exposure to objects at all levels of quality—seeing and handling a multitude of artifacts—along with a deliberate attempt to repeatedly draw comparisons between similar examples and make judgments regarding their relative merits, or the superiority of one over the other. A thorough knowledge of what constitutes quality in antiques acquired through reading and visiting museums and other public collections, and a good memory for what one has seen, will increase a collector's ability to make sound judgments through comparisons. Perhaps no person in the history of American antique collecting has been more renowned for possessing this sensitivity than Wallace Nutting, who, in his *Furniture Treasury* (1924), underlined the importance of this sometimes elusive quality: "In collecting one must either have some feeling for style or, merely desiring to be in fashion, must have the advice of one who does have that feeling."

Condition

If design quality and style are primary in creating the value and thus of affecting the price of an antique, then the *condition* of that object follows closely as an important consideration in establishing its worth. Regardless of its cost, no antique or collectible is worth having if it is in poor condition. A hairline crack in a spongeware pitcher, a chip on a Gallé vase, or a stain on the cover of a piece of sheet music, will never go away; it will always directly affect the optimum value of the piece. Even a repair well done affects the character and the price of an antique adversely. Not infrequently a pair of antique objects, identical but for their condition, have been auctioned sequentially. The perfect Mettlach stein, for example, may bring $225, while its mate, with a missing cover or cracked bottom, will sell for a fraction of that price. The auctioneer presiding at this event might, quite appropriately, remark that the imperfect piece has "a hundred-dollar crack"; this is a lesson worth remembering.

People collect for all kinds of reasons, and for some who collect, condition is unimportant. For those people who regularly buy damaged *shelf pieces*, whose flaws, however gross, do not show when they are displayed in their crowded vitrines and on overflowing tables and shelves, any education in matters of condition is wasted. However, the sophisticated collector will always regard the good condition of an object as an essential part of its integrity and its value, and will seek it first along with design quality and style.

Condition means many things to the wary collector, but it seldom implies that an antique should "look like new." The simple fact that an object has survived generations of use means that any expectation of a pristine condition must be tempered with a realistic view of what the vicissitudes of time and normal usage have done to its appearance. The older an object is, the greater likelihood that it has suffered greater alteration of its original state. But only the collectors of the earliest pieces such as Coptic textiles of the seventh century A.D. or of certain historic relics would be willing to accept objects in a fragmentary state. Those manufacturers who create modern furniture based on old styles, and then proceed to "stress" their surfaces by beating them with chains, shooting them with buckshot, or drilling them to create "worm holes," do a disservice even to these insensitive consumers by reinforcing the erroneous notion that "antique" somehow implies that a piece is in a state of decrepitude. No one buys genuine antiques because they are damaged by time; even less so should anyone buying new items fall for this ploy.

The buyer of antiques should always aspire to finding objects in as fine a condition as possible, whether their collecting specialty is tobacco tins, Art Deco atomizers, rose medallion porcelain, or tractor seats. One of the virtues of antiques over new goods of most kinds is that antiques will not only *hold* their value, but will usually *appreciate* with time. If a piece is damaged from the onset, this increase in worth will never happen. Major alterations of original condition affect the beauty of the piece as well. Advertisements announcing the offer of fine period furniture will often make reference to the state of preservation with such phrases as " . . . retaining its original golden color and surface," "A pair of blanket chests with original graining, hardware and cabinetwork," or " . . . outstanding condition and color."

The surfaces of old furniture, glass, ceramics, and metals, along with all other antiquities, possess a character usually referred to as *patina*. All objects reveal usage by the way in which their color, texture, or shape is altered with time. A copper roof or a bronze coin develops a familiar greenish hue from exposure to weather conditions or handling. A colonial silver teaspoon will be covered with minute scratches which alter its reflective qualities; its bowl may be worn flat on its left side from repeated scooping by generations of right-handed owners. The mahogany of a Sheraton chest of drawers will have a rich depth to its surface, particularly on its front and top, because of the successive layers of oil built up from the hands of those who used it and from particles in the atmosphere which have fallen on it. These normal alterations are expected (and sometimes desired) by collectors; they give important clues to a piece's authenticity.

Perhaps no subject relative to antique care is more controversial than that of refinishing. It is sufficient for the reader to know that natural patination is destroyed with the refinishing of a piece of furniture, and that equally destructive is the harsh and insensitive cleaning of old silver, bronze, pewter, and marble. The urge of collectors and dealers to want old things to look respectably clean and usable has taken its toll in the tens of thousands of pieces of furniture which have been "dipped and stripped" and the pewter which has been shined to look like stainless steel. On the other hand it is no pleasure to behold badly stained, scratched, and dented wood; the rubbing of wood with pumice or cleaning it with appropriate materials is preferable to stripping, sanding, and polyurethaning to make the old look new.

Beyond the patination of surface there are other factors of condition which need to be considered in judging the inherent value as well as the market value of an antique. Among these are the *completeness* of an object and the *originality* of its parts. Does an object have all of the parts original to it? An attractive, decorative Gouda pottery inkwell, otherwise perfect, may be missing its insert to hold the ink, or the original ceramic one has been replaced by one of glass. A Queen Anne highboy base, separated years earlier from its upper case of drawers, might be wedded with the top from another piece which has lost its bottom. This, appropriately, is called a *marriage*—a term which, in the trade, refers to the act of making a complete object from parts of several others. "Marriages" of other kinds are sometimes honestly described in dealer and auction catalog jargon as *assembled*. The phrase, "Chinese export assembled tea and coffee service, circa 1810," means that the various pieces of porcelain were not originally made to compose a single set, but rather pieces from various other incomplete sets were matched together at some later date by someone wishing to have a complete collection.

There is no good reason why collectors with sensitivity cannot perform their own assembling. Many a separated Art Nouveau glass lampshade has made its way to an appropriate bronze base through the intervention of a dealer or collector who knew what was originally *supposed* to go with what. Plenty of orphan glass inserts for Victorian caster sets have been matched up and fitted into silver stands which had lost their originals. In the larger sense, of course, all collecting is the reassembling of the past—historic restoration projects being the most visible, large-scale production of the sort.

The general shortage of good, early antiques for all those who desire to own them causes not only the assembling of matching sets to accommodate these markets, but also finds a considerable percentage of antiques on the market to be altered from their original state. This is particularly true of furniture, which is more easily repaired than glass, porcelain, or metal. The normal use of furniture, or anything else, causes eventual damage or loss to the original condition. Like a lost button on a coat, the loss of a handle on a chest of drawers may require the replacement of all the hardware rather than trying to find a match for the original. Replaced hardware is easily detected by examination of the patination (discoloration) around the handles on the front, and on the interior of the drawers by looking for signs of position change in the hardware (evidenced by new, or additional, holes and tampered wood surfaces).

An "assembled set" created by the collector may be more affordable than one made en suite by a single maker. These similar-looking pieces were made between 1892 and 1913 in three different English cities. "Assembled set" of English silver: coffee pot, Chester, 1901; tea pot, London, 1892; creamer, London, 1909; sugar, Birmingham, 1913. Rodney A. Schwartz collection. (Photo: Rodney A. Schwartz)

How much alteration from the original condition of a piece is acceptable to a collector or a dealer is largely a matter of personal taste. The upper-crust establishments who are the vendors of the greatest antiquities tolerate very little. "Minor repairs to the drawer edge," "Some interior repair," or even "a rich old finish" (which means *not* the original finish) are the usual caveats in their promotion of their inventory. Other dealers and collectors, less particular about total originality, will happily accept leaded-glass lamps with newly soldered replacement pieces, Oriental rugs with rewoven—or even missing—edges, a new drawer bottom on a pembroke table, or a 1910 wedding dress without the accompanying veil. Only a fool would dismiss the value of a Hepplewhite chest-on-chest because several backboards, or a leg, had been replaced. Change in the original integrity of any antique causes a lessening of its price. But because repair is a relative matter, every buyer needs to consider how much change is acceptable personally.

Curiously, dealers in some European countries, where a greater number of very early pieces are available, hold to unwritten, though broadly accepted, standards of what percentage of repairs and replacements are appropriate on a piece of antique furniture. In Holland, an antique needs to be only 40% original to pass as legitimate. In Denmark a figure closer to 60% is acceptable. Dealers who sell objects as antique when they do not meet these standards are, in fact, subject to legal action.

Unscrupulous dealers have been known to make deliberate alterations to antiques which are alien to their original condition for the sake of increasing their market value. This is called *embellishment* or *enhancement* of a piece. It is well known that a mahogany and satinwood Federal chest is more desirable if its apron contains an inlaid shell or fan motif, rather than being plain. An extra banded inlay along the top of a sewing table makes it more attractive. The plain, turned maple legs of a Sheraton table can be made to look like more desirable curly maple by spiralling a kerosene-soaked rope around them and briefly letting it burn to discolor the wood in a striped pattern. Curly maple also may be convincingly "created" by brushing diluted India ink in stripes across the grain of ordinary maple before it is varnished. All of these embellishments are easily accomplished relative to the increase in selling price which might be realized from the more elaborate piece.

There are certainly known cases of obliging older ladies who have innocently painted copper tea leaves onto easily found plain white nineteenth-century English stoneware on order from dealers who had a demand for the decorated tea leaf pattern which is much harder to find. Just as easy as painting tea leaves is the embellishment of plain salt-glazed stoneware crocks with cobalt decoration. The presence of a beautifully painted number, flower, bird, or, best of all, an American flag or an eagle, on an ordinary crock can boost its market price by hundreds of dollars. If a kiln is available, this task is simplicity itself, and well worth the trouble for those without conscience. Not a few bored dealers with nothing better to do have hand-colored early engravings with their box of watercolors, to accommodate contemporary tastes— even in full view of their confused customers.

Lamp repair shops have been known to remove the wired-on or soldered-on labels from a Tiffany or Handel lamp left by a customer, and place it on an unsigned lamp of their own to enhance its market appeal. Old paintings in the marketplace not only have had signatures added to increase their importance, but have had other pictorial features painted in to make an otherwise ordinary landscape, for example, more interesting with a couple more cows or peasants.

Uniqueness and Rarity

For many observers, uniqueness and rarity are synonymous with antiquity, though this is not supported in fact. Regardless of how precious they may seem to their owners, Wedgwood jasperware, Mason's ironstone, Currier and Ives prints, Haviland china, and pressed pattern glass were manufactured by the thousands or even millions of pieces when they were new. At the time of their creation, they were neither unique (the only one ever made) nor were they rare (unplentiful). Today most of these pieces are still quite common, and their relatively modest market prices reflect their plentiful supply. Some of these pieces have *become* less common through the damage and loss to others of their kind in the intervening years—but few are rare; none, probably, are unique.

Uniqueness in the antique market is always problematic. Because the value and to some extent the significance of a work of art or an antique is usually based upon its *comparative* relationship with other similar examples, an object of singular character of which only one was ever produced—or survives—poses problems for both seller and buyer in establishing its "correct price." In the improbable event that the magnificent (and unique) gold salt cellar once owned by Francis I—the only extant and documented work by Renaissance goldsmith Benvenuto Cellini—were suddenly to appear on the market, it would be virtually impossible to assign a price to it. Likewise, settling on a figure that adequately reflected the value of Michelangelo's only signed work, the *Pietà*, a piece of furniture proven to be from the hand of Thomas Chippendale himself (none are yet certain to be by him), or the Dead Sea Scrolls, would be a challenging task indeed.

In circles outside the marketplace, one frequently hears the phrase "priceless antiques," a meaningless term if there ever was one. No object, even unique like Cellini's masterpiece, is without a price which someone would be willing to pay for it, and the price for great and rare objects is determined when they hit the market, usually within the forum of a public auction. Observing the appreciating value of unique objects is a fascinating, if largely academic, pursuit. The 1856 British Guiana one-cent stamp, printed because of an emergency shortage, and in the wrong color, is universally regarded as the world's rarest postage stamp. It is, for all intents and purposes, unique, as no others of its kind have ever been identified. The stamp, originally worth only a penny, was sold in 1872 to a local dealer in Georgetown, British Guiana, for six shillings. After the First World War, the stamp was sold for $32,500, and again in 1970 for $284,000. Ten years later its sale brought over $1 million.

Rarity alone will not guarantee a high value to any given object. Some artifacts which might accurately be described as unique still have little monetary value because they lack the more important qualities of innate beauty, historical significance, or desirability. The only quilt ever made by one's own great-grandmother, or a singular hand-carved wooden leg owned by a seventeenth-century pirate, however unique, would probably not realize an enormous auction price because it has a limited market appeal. For most collectors, the potential for discovering an object which can truly be called "unique" is slim. Even if such an object were to be found, the chance of recognizing its significance without a basis for comparison would be equally remote.

Rarity, rather than uniqueness, might more properly be a concern for an experienced collector. While *uniqueness* refers to one, *rarity* may be used to describe the supply of several or even many similar objects. A case in point would be a Gutenberg Bible. In the fifteenth century the German printer Johannes Gutenberg developed moveable type and an edition of 185 Bibles, believed to have been printed at least in part by him, was produced. To date 48 copies are known to exist. The discovery of additional copies, or the appearance of a copy on the market, always generates considerable interest and speculation as to what it might bring. In 1975 the 48th copy was found by a school teacher rummaging through the attic of a German pastor. At the time, it was appraised at $3.2 million and donated to a museum. Subsequent sales of known copies have brought even more, such as the one sold in 1987 for $5.39 million. Other fifteenth-century religious books, printed in even fewer numbers, may never achieve this price. Gutenberg Bibles in general are valuable because they are *rare* and *historically significant* (because they were the *first* books printed with the newly discovered moveable type). The most recently sold copy was specifically valuable because, unlike many of the other surviving versions, it was in pristine condition, its pages clean and fresh, and in its original Mainz binding.

Pilgrim furniture, almost by virtue of its definition, is rare, because so little of it was made for the then meager population of America. Trestle tables, chair tables, press cupboards, and Brewster chairs made before 1700 are so few that most are in museums, and, in the rare instances when they are offered on the market, they rightly are subject to the greatest scrutiny before very high prices are paid for them. Furniture from the hand, or even from the workshop, of an identifiable eighteenth-century cabinetmaker is nearly always considered to be rare. Over several generations, one of the great firms, Townsend and Goddard of Newport, Rhode Island, produced superlative pieces of distinctively designed and crafted furniture. While several hundred pieces made by the firm are still extant, almost any one of them will bring a fine price. In 1985 the highest price ever paid at auction for a piece of American furniture was a Townsend and Goddard kneehole block-front desk which brought $375,000. Of these desks there are only a handful, and most are owned by public museums.

Rarity, of course, considers not only how many objects were originally made which yet remain, but also how many are *available* on the market. There are, for example, several hundred Rembrandt paintings in museums (thus they are not rare in the sense of numbers), but more appropriately affecting their market value is the fact that very few still reside in private collections. Since museums owning Rembrandts are unlikely to sell them, the only ones of consequence to the potential buyer (which will probably be another museum) are those few still in private hands, which, someday, may be sold. Pre-Reformation English silver, Renaissance costumes, or classical sculpture also fall into similar categories of lack of availability, and thus command high prices.

On the few occasions when it is applicable, dealers in fine furniture refer to the rarity of pieces they have for sale. An ad may read, "One of three known blanket chests of this type from Schwaben Creek Valley, Pennsylvania," " . . . rare William and Mary maple and ash round-top tavern table," or even "A rare and possibly unique Hepplewhite grain-painted maple and pine console table." In the various descriptions of items the rarity may refer to that of provenance, shape, or decoration, as in the three preceding examples. Certain quite common objects become valuable if they are variations or aberrations from the majority of those produced.

While there are tens of thousands of mustache cups from the period 1880–1910 (as well as many hundreds of collectors of them), a very small percentage of these cups are left-handed ones. Even the circumstance of being left handed in the past century was considered by many to be a social and moral stigma, and mustache cups deliberately crafted for left-handed customers are a distinct rarity. Even rarer are silver mustache spoons. Violins by Italian masters Antonio Stradivari or Joseph Guarneri have brought record-breaking prices, over $200,000 in some instances. No matter how productive, violin makers, like furniture makers, produce only so many works in a lifetime, and the relatively few masterpieces among them bring the highest prices to buyers who can discriminate between the ordinary and the superlative.

Two Red Wing stoneware pitchers from the same period (c. 1914), factory, and mold have very different market values because of the rarity of one caused by the advertising it bears. Author's collection. (Photo: Jim Barbour)

Provenance

Numberless are the estate sales and auctions to which novices flock because the worldly goods or excess baggage (sometimes quite literally) of some political luminary, underworld figure, or movie star are being sold to the public. In the minds of these people, ordinary objects such as a golf ball, a set of clubs, or a pipe are transformed into relics of special significance because they were owned by Bing Crosby. A tea set owned by Adolf Hitler, adorned with eagles, swastikas, and the initials "A.H.," draws crowds at an auction. Likewise, General Douglas MacArthur's 1942 Packard was sold in 1979 for $150,000. Other golf balls, silver services, and Packards not owned by celebrities do not enjoy these inflated prices, and their sales regularly go unnoticed.

In 1976 a monogrammed pair of drawers, and another in 1977, once owned by Queen Victoria were sold for $107 and $280 respectively. On a higher plane, when the much-awaited public auction of the Duchess of Windsor's legendary jewelry collection finally took place in 1987, even the distinguished auction house doing the sale was astounded by the prices which individual pieces brought. Of considerable interest to observers of this event was the fact that, almost without exception, the great jewels realized figures very close to their estimates, whereas less important pieces with engraved sentiments brought prices many times their predicted levels—or their intrinsic merit, for that matter. Ownership of a personal token which was a gift of King Edward VIII to the woman he loved, is, apparently, worth more than its weight in gold.

Provenance refers to the origin or source of an object. In broader definition, it is the history of the ownership of an object. *Who* owned an object *can* be an appropriate and legitimate reason for an increase in its market value, though it is almost always linked with some other factor affecting worth, such as beauty or historic importance. In perusing the best auction catalogs, one frequently finds reference to former owners in the description of single lots or entire collections; indeed, auction houses seem to prefer offering for sale items which have belonged in the collections of the great. "From the collection of Mrs. Francis P. Garvan, Jr.," " . . . the collection of Colonel Edgar William and Bernice Chrysler Garbish, New York," and " . . . the property of the Duke of Devonshire" are typical of the kinds of references to ownership which are found with regularity. If anonymity is requested by the vendor, or if the seller does not have an easily recognized name, the descriptive line simply may state "The property of a Lady" or "The property of a Gentleman."

A rare Queen Anne highboy, sold by John Walton Inc. in 1987, was advertised in the following way: "Written on a fragment of a revolutionary War Military Pass glued inside a drawer are the names Jesse Birchard and Norwich." The Birchard family was one of the original settlers of Norwich, Connecticut. In addition to the highboy itself, representing the highest form of Connecticut cabinetmaking, this provenance enriches its connections with history. Likewise, a pair of Queen Anne chairs sold by a Massachusetts firm, described as the Gov. Gideon Wanton Chairs, were characterized as follows: "These chairs were part of the furnishings of the Nichols-Wanton-Hunter House and descended directly through the family until recently purchased by us." The establishment of provenance for some objects is exceedingly important; with regularity, museums investigate the ownership of their works of art. The best provenance for a painting, for example, is to be able to trace it directly to the artist's studio in which it was created. The legendary and mysterious portrait popularly referred to as Mona Lisa is one of the few paintings by the artist known to have been in the possession of Leonardo da Vinci at the time of his death.

For some buyers, there is a certain assurance in knowing that the antiquity being sold belonged to someone renowned for having a collection of quality; it is an immediate pedigree. For other buyers, a famous name alone connected with a piece, regardless of its quality, is enough to give it distinction and desirability. In 1980, within five minutes after the bidding opened at $36,000, a mahogany bed decorated with bronze ormolu mounts of Venus and Cupid and a Napoleonic eagle was sold at auction in Berne, Switzerland, for $126,000. The piece was reputed to have been a "Wedding Bed" made for Napoleon Bonaparte. With a provenace equally distinctive, a pair of delicately decorated Sèvres porcelain milk pails made for Marie Antoinette was sold in 1978 for a record Sèvres price of $102,600. To assuage her ennui, it seems, the bored queen dressed in a peasant costume and gamboled about the lawn pretending to be a milkmaid. In 1982 a pair of pistols of supreme quality was found in the New York City police property warehouse along with other illegal weapons. Their quality, and the initials inlaid in gold, indicated that they had been made by the eighteenth-century imperial gunmaker Johan Adolph Grecke for his empress, Catherine the Great. Upon being given to the Metropolitan Museum, they were estimated to be worth $200,000. Described as "true works of art," clearly their quality, as well as the distinction of their ownership, was important in establishing their high value. A home movie, distinguished from all others because it was taken for fun by the Beatles while they were making a professional film, brought thousands of dollars beyond its estimate in a 1987 auction.

1988 proved to be another year of record prices for objects having belonged to celebrities. On the final day of a four-day auction of the partial contents of Liberace's various plush domiciles, the entertainer's driver's license, forecast to garner no more than $200, went for $4,150. Similarly the estate of pop artist Andy Warhol was auctioned amid a frenzy of interest from the art world as well as popular culture devotees. The hype surrounding the auction made national television news and a *Newsweek* cover entitled "Art for Money's Sake." The illustrated six-volume catalog of the Warhol auction, itself now a collector's item, was available for $95. Of all the unexpectedly high prices realized at the sale, perhaps the most memorable was that achieved by the artist's rather random collection of 1950s cookie jars. Lot number 838, listed as four American cookie jars, estimated to sell for $100–200, was actually sold for $11,550. Another lot of miscellaneous cookie jars, some incomplete, brought $12,100, exactly $12,000 more than the low estimate established by the auction house. It should be stressed that identical versions of virtually any of these jars could be purchased in antique shops and flea markets across the country for $27.50 apiece. It is unlikely that the enthusiastic buyer of this lot could turn around and sell the same collection at any time in the future for a figure even remotely approaching the one he or she paid.

Historical Significance

In the case of famous owners, it is difficult to separate the person who owned an object from its historical significance. Clearly anything which was owned by Louis XIV, including his chamberpot, would have some historical importance by virtue of the fact that he was king of France. It is also difficult to determine what part *ownership* and *quality* each plays in the evaluation of the fine property of a powerful figure. A Louis XIV chamberpot, like a pair of pistols of the Tsarina, is likely to have been made better, and more distinctively, because it was specifically intended for a person of importance; thus its price is affected. The items listed in the previous section, owned by famous people, take on additional significance because they are documents of the historical periods from which they come. Few objects, or even written descriptions of the period, for example, could reveal as poignantly the corrupted state of the French aristocracy in the last days of the monarchy as the hand-painted porcelain milk pails of Marie Antoinette.

In the fall of 1988, a pair of ruby slippers believed to have been worn by Judy Garland in *The Wizard of Oz*, and also known to collectors of Hollywood memorabilia as the "witch's shoes," was privately sold by Christie's for $165,000. The cult followers of Judy Garland and

Oz artificially created this unrealistic price unrelated to the actual value of the shoes.

Some objects are valuable *solely* because they have historical significance, and not because of any intrinsic qualities of beauty or worth which they might possess. Most documents on paper which testify to the interactions of people and nations fall into this category. The several versions of Lincoln's Gettysburg Address or of the Magna Carta, the original manuscript for Lewis Carroll's *Alice's Adventures under Ground,* or the Declaration of Independence are familiar examples. The value of the spontaneous home movie of Abraham Zapruder, who happened to have his camera operating in Dallas on November 22, 1963, when John F. Kennedy's motorcade passed by, is entirely due to its historical and documentary nature and not to its artistry. George Washington's several sets of false teeth, now enjoying museum settings, are similarly significant because of their place in history. Objects of this kind, however, cannot be categorized strictly as "antiques" in the sense in which the term is used throughout this book.

If it were not so important a feature of Great Britain's history, the chair upon which all the kings and queens of England have been crowned since 1296 would be worth no more than any other piece of Gothic furniture if its value were based entirely upon its physical features. The chair in which Abraham Lincoln was shot at Ford's Theater is no different from hundreds of other Victorian chairs which are regularly sold for a few hundred dollars, except for its unfortunate role in our nation's history. Historical societies and museums throughout the country are the repositories for ordinary objects which have been given more than ordinary attention because of their presence in some memorable event. "The first softball," "Part of the rigging of the Mayflower," or "Glasses worn by an early Methodist," are typical labels found in museums to justify the presence of otherwise common things behind glass. For decades, the Hennepin County Historical Society in Minneapolis displayed a caned rocker of a usual late Victorian sort with the sinister label, "A Murderer Sat In This Chair." Handsome Harry Hayward, who had paid to have his female creditor murdered in 1895, apparently spent a few anxious moments in this chair while waiting to be hanged. The object was seized by witnesses and preserved (along with the handcuffs which manacled him and a piece of the rope which hanged him) as valuable because of its connection with the grim event.

The link with history is a consideration in buying an antique which is not without its pitfalls. The collector needs to remember that *all* objects are connected with history, but many are not associated with world-changing, unusual, or even curious events. Regrettably, most objects have become dissociated from their stories through the passage of time. For this very reason, many collectors have lamented the fact that their antiques could not "talk" to reveal their stories. The danger for collectors in ascribing undue importance to the historical value of an object is to miss the most important reason for its ownership—its inherent worth and the beauty of the object itself and what it tells of society in a broader sense. Auctioneers, dealers, and those who sell privately delight in conveying specific historical legends about the objects they are vending to increase their appeal to the buyer. They are regularly armed with phrases such as, "I bought it from a very wealthy banker in Atlanta," "It came out of a seventeenth-century house in Salem," or "This bugle was played at the dedication of the Washington Monument." The tiny Mayflower could never have accommodated all the objects attributed to its cargo, to say nothing of all the people whose later ancestors have claimed their passage on the same. The worth of an antique must be judged first by what it is and not upon who owned it or where it was used. Historical information enriches the appreciation of objects, but cannot compensate for other qualities which are missing.

Pairs and Complete Sets

Objects made in multiples, intended from their origins to be pairs or sets, whose companion pieces still exist, are more valuable than equal numbers of comparable individual examples. Candlesticks, dueling pistols, flatware, dining chairs, salt casters, and garniture, almost without exception, were made this way. In addition, many vases, figurines, and pieces of bedroom and dining-room furniture were originally made to be in pairs or *en suite*. An eighteenth-century pair of Chelsea figures of a shepherd and shepherdess commands a price more than double that of either separate piece. The intact nature of pairs or sets is directly related to *condition* in antique collecting. Recognizing this fact, many insurance companies allow full compensation in a claim, even if only one of a pair of items is lost. Naturally, they also have the right of possession of the remaining piece after the monetary settlement.

The desirability of complete sets mentioned earlier is such that many collectors attempt to re-create them from components found here and there. While this kind of assembled collection is a legitimate pursuit, the desire for creating "sets" sometimes goes beyond the bounds of good taste, reason, or legality. One such illustration should suffice in alerting the antique collector to be cautious when buying sets. A set of four American Queen Anne side chairs, for example, would be a delight for even the most discriminating collector to own. But a set of six would be infinitely better, and a set of eight, nearly divine. A dishonest vendor, possessing some skill and nerve, could create a set of six chairs from four by reassembling their parts and replacing some of each original chair with enough new, faked pieces to create two additional chairs with some genuine parts. The task of actually doing this would be considerable, but, if successfully accomplished, the effort would be well rewarded in the difference of cash realized between four and six

A pair of Gouda earthenware vases (c. 1930) are made more desirable and valuable because they are a matched pair, fully signed on the bottom, and both retain their original paper labels. Dutch tin-glazed vases, Gouda, the Netherlands. Goldstein Gallery, gift of Leona A. Schwab in memory of Prof. and Mrs. Elvin Stakman. (Photo: Judy Olausen, courtesy of Goldstein Gallery)

matching eighteenth-century chairs. More commonly found in the trade than fraudulently re-created sets are sets of chairs which are assembled by gathering together very similar, though not absolutely matched, examples. A very careful inspection of finish, proportion, and profile will reveal this fact. Sets of chairs, incidentally, are frequently numbered under their slip seats with a Roman numeral. If someone is selling a "set" of chairs which have nonconsecutive numbers, it is a certainty that the set originally contained more pieces which are now missing.

Signatures and Dates

There is little disagreement that the presence of a signature or date on a work of art or an antique does have some bearing on its evaluation. Whether it *should* or not is probably open to some discussion. If we didn't know who wrote, composed, or painted anything, we might be better able to appreciate every artistic work more rightly for its own merits. The world of antiques has its heroes. For collectors of eighteenth-century objects the hero might be Gainsborough, Herold, or Wedgwood; for the nineteenth century, Landseer, William Morris, or Louis Comfort Tiffany; to collectors of the twentieth century, the names of Picasso, Frank Lloyd Wright, and Charles Eames are synonymous with greatness in the objects they created. It is only natural, then, that many sellers of antiques wish to link their objects with the perceived glory of these heroic figures. In this feeble pursuit, many a naive dealer has shown an even more gullible buyer a picture from a book on fine antiques, which bore only the vaguest relationship to the piece they were selling, and claimed it to be "just like it." When antiques and works of art not only resemble accepted great examples, but possess signatures and dates, their credentials seem complete—they have a pedigree, a specific identity.

Much to the chagrin of collectors and dealers, most antiques are neither signed nor dated. Objects made in their time as utilitarian props, regardless of the interest or artistry perceived in them by later admirers, were not considered important enough to document with a name, place, or date connected with their manufacture. Those who specialize in collecting artist-decorated Rookwood pottery, English silver, or certain American coverlets are fortunate that both signatures and dates are nearly always present—imbedded in the object; other collectors are not so lucky. Authorship, age, and other matters regarding the origin of most antiques must be deduced from the objects themselves—from their style and condition. Some kinds of antiques are more likely to be signed than others. Potters seem to sign their work more frequently than some other craftsmen—perhaps because it is so easy to scratch into the damp clay or brush on with the glaze. The appearance of a signed piece of furniture on the market is such a rarity that it almost always causes dealers to make specific reference to it in their advertising. A tall-case clock might be described as " . . . bearing its original paper label"; a chest of drawers, "Signed in four places by the maker"; or a Renaissance revival sofa frame, "Signed in chalk on the seat rail, 'Jelliff." An inordinate dependence upon signatures to confirm quality in antiques or works of art may lead a collector to overlook more important features, or, indeed, to ignore the possibility that the signature is a forgery.

Ordinary unsigned late eighteenth-century American silver spoons have occasionally later been stamped with the name "REVERE" to make them saleable for a price hundreds of dollars more than they might otherwise have commanded. In the days when skilled labor was cheaper, the entire center of a damaged silver tray (with family crest on one side and hallmarks on the other), or the bottom of an irreparable sterling teapot stamped with good hallmarks, were removed and cleverly joined to similar vessels which had less distinguished marks. To the unwary buyer, they would appear to be worth much more because of their better hallmarks. Apparently the market contained enough novice buyers, who depended on the markings rather than the total integrity of a piece to determine its authenticity, that frauds of this sort were easily placed in their hands.

Falsified signatures on paintings are found in museums as well as in private collections with some regularity. Many pictures of the seventeenth century, including some genuine Rembrandts, bear false Rembrandt signatures because someone at one time thought it would give the object—even the real one—greater credibility. All other factors being equal (which they seldom are), a genuine signature on a genuine painting is a good thing to have, but it probably affects price relatively little. Many of the greatest paintings and sculptures of the world are unsigned. Mediocre works of art are not worth having, regardless of whose signature they possess. The authenticity of paintings is established by their comparison with other documented works and their stylistic and thematic consistency with other known works. And like the value of any other antiquity, true value is inherent in its design and the competence of its execution—not in who did or did not sign it.

Sometimes the presence of a signature or date on an object is misleading in judging its true identity. In antique collecting one occasionally comes across an object of genuine antiquity which bears embellishment—decoration, date, or name—added sometime *after* the piece itself was made. Typical instances in which this is likely to occur might be on a Norwegian immigrant trunk, an eighteenth-century German glass beaker, or a silver teapot. A Scandinavian trunk might easily have been made in the late eighteenth century; and, when a family member decided to emigrate to America in the 1870s, the piece was then painted with the traveler's name, point of destination, and date. Likewise, a certain percentage of such items as a Germanic handblown *Waldglasbecker* (or beaker), many of which were intended to remain plain, were decorated a century later, when they were more appreciated, with colored enamel flowers, armorial themes, or dates, by someone who realized their greater market appeal. Other old glass, and certainly many pieces of silver, have had perfectly legitimate inscriptions engraved on them later for the occasion of a baptism, marriage, or anniversary presentation. Engraved silver, after it leaves the possession of the unfamiliar family or organization for whom it was personalized, actually becomes less valuable on the market. There would be few interested buyers, for example, for even a fine Victorian silver teapot if it bore the inscription "To the Reverend Cecil Clark on the Occasion of the Fortieth Anniversary of his Pastorate at St. Stephen's." Thus, many an engraved sentiment has been removed from the face of a piece of silver by hammering and polishing until it is no more. The removal, however, is seldom entirely invisible, and a clever silver buyer by fogging the surface with breath should be able to reveal momentarily the ghost of any engraving which remains almost imperceptible.

Antiques which once bore signatures may no longer hold them because of later circumstances. Many a legitimate signature on a painting has disappeared when the picture was vigorously overcleaned. Paper labels which once identified the manufacturer of art glass and art pottery have dried out and fallen off by the thousands. Both Handel and Tiffany lamps were sometimes marked by cloth labels glued to the felt padding of their bases and have come unglued. Signatures and dates may easily come and go from antiques or fakes, and the wary collector should base the decision to purchase a piece first on its quality and condition, and last on whether or not it is signed.

Popularity

There are few greater pleasures for the antique collector than being able to buy something at a good price because no one else recognizes, understands, or appreciates it for its true value. The reason that this happens less often than one would hope is, in part, because the history of antique collecting, along with the marketing of any other commodity, is heavily affected by the popularity of the items being vended; most people collect popular, mainstream artifacts and most collectors follow, rather than set, trends. Many people imagine that antiques, the very symbols of continuity, stability, and conservatism, are exempt from the caprices of public taste and the whims of popularity. However, merely sitting quite regularly through auctions held over a period of several years will alert the collector to the fact that antiques also enjoy periods of popular approval, as well as ones of public coolness or even scorn.

The interest in some antiques and collectibles is almost seasonal. The same wicker furniture which prompts frantic bidding in the spring and early summer may be met by a winter crowd with considerable indifference. Old stained-glass windows and brass beds were so popular in the 1960s and '70s that no dealer could keep enough of them in stock. Such was the frenzy for decorative windows that many a dealer at the time was offered stolen ones, ripped from their original settings to supply a market so demanding that even thieves were aware of it. Since the growing affection for both stained glass and brass beds, prompted in part by eclectic decorating trends shown in popular magazines, could not meet the available supply of genuine ones, even new reproductions moved in to fill the gap. Today neither stained glass nor brass beds are nearly as popular as they once were. Like golden oak furniture, their time came and went (and will likely come again), and some dealers, entering the market too late, got stuck having paid top dollar for inventory once popular, which they could not sell to an audience with waning interest.

Observing the importance of popularity of certain kinds of antiques in the market over many years and even decades is even more instructive than seeing the short run. In March, 1980, the *New York Times* published a chart which tracked the favorites in American furniture over every decade of the twentieth century. Ratings of popularity were described in five stages: peaking, popular, gaining, emerging, and unwanted. The study, based on the tracking of auction prices for single or related pieces, indicated that at the turn of the century, pilgrim furniture was at its height. In 1920, furniture from the William and Mary period enjoyed its greatest appreciation to date, and Federal furniture first peaked then. The appeal of Queen Anne and Chippendale has either gradually risen or leveled off in the last eighty years, without major slumps. It is perhaps not surprising that the simple furniture made by the utopian Shaker communities, first appearing on the national market about 1930, had its highest peak of popularity in the 1960s when the nation saw peace rallies, the return to the earth movement, and an increased interest in ecology and natural foods. Large sections of the country, it seems, were exhibiting a temperament with spiritual ties to Shaker beliefs of simplicity and concord (though not the less popular celibacy). The *Times* study shows the late entrance into the market of the more recent styles of the golden oak era (1945), arts and crafts (1956), and Art Deco (1972). If the price and availability of American period furniture, now a constant feature of the inventory of the greatest dealers, can have been affected by popularity, then it is safe to assume that lesser items are even more vulnerable to the uncertainties of fad or fashion.

On an entirely different level, the interest in collecting baseball cards has seen an enormous growth of popularity among hobbyists. In 1978 there were forty stores throughout the United States which more or less exclusively limited their business to the selling of such cards. By 1987 this figure had multiplied to over 1,000 shops. Certainly the increased interest in professional sports teams, and the continuing production and availability of cards which featured emerging sports superstars, is in large part responsible for such market reaction to something which might be viewed as an investment vehicle.

The international picture trade, which deals in paintings, drawings, and prints, is affected not only by the popularity of the work of certain artists, but curiously by the popularity of the *subjects* they have depicted. The art historian who views pictures does so with an eye for the quality of the art itself, for its style, beauty, and competence of execution. The possible obscurity, or even the disagreeable nature of the subject is largely irrelevant. For scholars, themes such as *The Blessed Transportation of the House of Levi, Jael and Sisera*, or *The Flaying of Marsyius*, have little bearing on a picture's intrinsic merits, and may even act to further pique their interest because of the arcane subject.

Dealers, however, view things differently. Antique dealers appropriately handle pictures which the public likes; they seek art with popular themes and agreeable subjects which are not disturbing to viewers. They want landscapes, flower paintings, and portraits of attractive people, preferably young and well-dressed. This is a tendency not usually found in sales galleries which deal exclusively in fine art. But it is nearly endemic among antique dealers, who, almost universally, are confused when confronting original art and are incapable of discerning its value beyond the clues provided by signature or subject matter. Most antique dealers know that religious images represented in pictures, sculpture, figurines, or in other artifacts, do not sell well, and that pictures of obscure saints or martyrdoms make even religious people nervous. They also know that, even if equal in quality, pictures of horses sell better than pictures of cows; that male nudes, because they are rarer, often bring more money from certain buyers, though female nudes appeal to a larger mainstream audience. Once clothed, however, portraits of women sell better because of their more interesting costume features. Among studio paintings, pictures of flowers have more buyers than still lifes with dead rabbits. For the connoisseur of pictures, capable of determining quality and authenticity, the buying of paintings, drawings, and prints can bring both aesthetic and monetary rewards. Few are the antique dealers who really understand pictures, and many overlook their true merit. Thus the practice of specializing for the collector, once again, gives an advantage to the painting or print connoisseur over the vendor.

The popularity of certain kinds of antiques is often subject to regional as well as global variations. Collectors who are familiar with the international picture know that objects are often most appreciated in the country of their origin. Collectibles related to the British royal family, for example, are most dearly prized (and priced) in England, while these same items have many fewer interested buyers in the United States. Naturally, the plentiful supply makes antiques of some kinds popular. In the eastern part of this country, which has a lengthier history, Federal furniture is collected with great regularity because it is both familiar and available. But in the midwest, or even west, where early furniture is scarce, oak furniture originally distributed by the catalog houses from 1900 to 1920 is much more recognized, has many devotees, and brings high prices.

What *causes* antiques to be popular is a subject which should be of considerable interest to the collector. Popularity seems to be generally unaffected by the actual potential supply of the item itself. For generations, art historians have known that art prices increase dramatically with new scholarship written to give new focus to a particular artist or school. Articles in scholarly journals, and even complete monographs, have brought artists of sometimes well-deserved obscurity into the light of day, and consequently their sale prices are affected positively. Clever historians have been known to quietly assemble private caches of works by "their man" and then publish the definitive essay on him, happily sitting back to watch their own collection appreciate by virtue of their research, writing, and their intuition. The rising prices in recent years of the works of Mannerist painters, or of the Pre-Raphaelites, or even of certain commercial illustrators of the last century are instances of appreciation attributed directly to new scholarship and the accompanying reappraisal of their significance in the art world. The rest of the antique market is similarly affected, and the importance of publications in transmitting enthusiasm for an area of collecting cannot be overstated.

New books, continually being published, define yet some new specialty that can be collected. Sometimes these sources will identify a particular designer or design firm (Chase Art Deco metal work, Gouda pottery, Heisey glass, Red Wing pottery). Other books explain a style: Adirondack furniture, folk art, or fabulous '50s. Some writers on antiques present their material thematically, bringing attention and meaning to the examples they have gathered (historic ironing devices, Antique Builders' hardware, American pocket watches). Popular home-furnishing and decorating magazines and the great antique collecting journals are influential in promoting a style, a period, or "a look."

Exhibitions, major and minor, in museums nationwide, usually accompanied by superb, scholarly publications, have an important impact on collecting and dealing audiences. A Metropolitan Museum exhibit of Fortuni fabrics and costumes sends market prices of those items sky high. Likewise, exhibits of Amish quilts, Latvian mittens, de Stijl, or even Herman Miller furniture sensitize the public to the identity, characteristics, significance, and value of these new arenas of collecting. High-quality sales galleries frequently act deliberately to affect the market they have cornered by (1) accumulating many works by an unknown artist, (2) writing a comprehensive catalog of biographical and artistic information, and (3) then holding an exhibition and sale of the newly discovered works. Invariably other pictures done by the same artist come to light and their owners profit from the earlier exposure (and recent education) which the sponsoring gallery promoted. The popularity and high prices of Fulper pottery and the increasing attention to California and southwest regionalist painters can be attributed to marketing efforts such as this.

The advent of the Bicentennial in this country intensified the interest by many Americans in their own roots and in their ethnic heritages. In turn, this has caused the searching for documentation of all manner of subjects, the writing of family histories, and an intense preoccupation with the material objects which link one generation with another. Artifacts connected with the Native American and Black populations, for example, have become increasingly visible on the market and are commanding ever rising prices as the cultures they represent are rediscovered and appreciated.

The collector who has the foresight, intelligence, and independence to identify and confidently accumulate objects of quality for which there is not yet a visible, popular market is the one who has the best chance of doing well in the antique game if he or she also possesses patience.

7

THE CARE OF A COLLECTION

Lay not up for yourselves treasures upon earth,
where moth and rust doth corrupt, and where
thieves break through and steal.

Gospel of St. Matthew VI:19

The monumental amount of time, money, intelligence, and affection which typically constitutes the formation of a good collection makes the additional effort required to protect what one already has seem minimal by comparison. If collectors follow the general rule of only buying antiques in good condition, then the only major concern in their care should be the *prevention* of damage. Even if entirely aware of the deleterious effects to which antiques are subject, no one who collects, not even museums, is able to control every potentially harmful factor. Yet, the proper care of antiques need not be a full-time job; it requires only the application of some relatively simple guidelines to minimize their deterioration or prevent their loss, through time, ignorance, or neglect.

Heat and Humidity

The combined qualities of the environment itself—temperature, humidity, light, and impurities—form one of the great hazards to preserving objects in their original pristine condition. The constant cold of the arctic ice and the dry heat of the desert sands have been responsible for sustaining the products of man and nature for millennia, yet the *alternating* effects of heat and cold found in many climates, sometimes as much as 140 degrees between seasons, can be fatal to some objects. The advent of central heating in the late nineteenth century, while a boon to human inhabitants, introduced additional problems for the care of antiques, particularly of furniture, as it seriously reduces the humidity levels.

Antique furniture, textiles, and art on paper or canvas are the collectibles most susceptible to the adverse effects of temperature change. Wood, fabric, and paper have their own moisture content, but also have the capacity for absorption or emission of moisture in relation to the environment in which they are placed. Particularly damaging to objects made of these materials are the dramatic *changes* of temperature and humidity to which they are regularly subjected. The insensitive and often irrational placement of heat registers, radiators, and air-conditioning vents in many houses makes the collector's job of interior planning a difficult one, particularly where the long-term preservation of objects is being considered. Furniture should *never* be placed directly next to, or in the path of, heat or cold from any source. Furniture which is overheated dries out and consequently splits, glue desiccates, joints loosen, veneer pops up, and the finish itself may crackle to an alligator surface.

A rise in furnace heat causes a corresponding reduction of moisture content, unless humidifying equipment has been added. The ideal relative humidity for wood is 50–55%, though most private residences are unable to achieve such optimum levels. Maintaining a 30–40% level is usually sufficient for the average collector to prevent serious problems. Collectors who live in northern climates often utilize separate humidifiers in the winter months to slow and reduce the dramatic seasonal differences in humidity fluctuations. Vulnerable objects, of course, should also be protected from direct contact with the emissions of humidifiers. It is nothing short of miraculous that so many antiques in relatively good condition have been discovered lurking in attics which are notorious for both their intense heat and cold in the changing seasons.

If dry heat is damaging, dampness is no less so. Collectors living in constantly damp climates must maintain vigilance particularly in the preservation of textiles, paper, and corrodible metals where regular ventilation and occasional airing of property is essential. Extreme dampness harbors mildew, fungus, and odors; encourages dry rot and rust; loosens glue; buckles paper; and warps wood. Basements—the repositories for the lesser property of almost every American family—are the spaces where most collectors find problems caused by moisture. It is therefore prudent to avoid *ever* storing certain kinds of artifacts there. Paper goods, books, textiles of any kind, upholstered furniture, and paintings or other framed works of art are best stored elsewhere. In addition to the damage caused by the moisture itself, damp environments attract silverfish, roaches, termites, firebrats, crickets, millipedes, centipedes, and spiders, which can destroy objects by eating glue, paper, wood, or cloth. Good ventilation, cleanliness, and periodic inspection are the best ways to prevent such problems, and prevention is more easily achieved than restoration.

The use of dehumidifiers will help to alleviate damp conditions, but they must be tended regularly and, unlike humidifiers, they take generous amounts of power to operate. Deliquescents such as silica gel (often packed in small sacks with new cameras or scientific instruments) and larger bags of calcium chloride are sometimes used to absorb excess moisture in relatively small areas, but unless care is taken to prevent their direct contact with artifacts, or to remove them immediately when they become saturated, they are more harmful than they are beneficial.

Light

Direct or indirect sunlight can be an immediate and fast-working danger to all manner of materials. For generations, dry-goods merchants have known how quickly textiles can fade in a store window, and they regularly have used awnings. For private collectors, pictures on the wall, upholstery, rugs, or even furniture are no less vulnerable to the damaging action of light. They will do well to observe how major modern museums are designed to admit no natural light where certain kinds of collections are shown. Likewise the collector can place watercolors, prints, drawings, and textiles away from direct light, which shockingly is sometimes capable of fading objects within a few days. Nearly every estate sale reveals at least one occasional table with a dark, circular spot in the center where a lamp sat for several decades, while all the wood around it is faded by the action of the sun through the window. The harsh effects of sunlight can be reduced by adjusting blinds, or even by coating certain windows with ultra-violet-screening film.

Artificial light also poses dangers to certain kinds of materials. The heat of incandescent lamps at close distances to artifacts may cause excessive drying; this action sometimes takes place almost imperceptibly over many years. A fashion among art collectors of some years ago, fortunately less popular these days, was the use of small lamps directly attached to the frames of pictures. Many a venerated old oil painting bears the scars of dried, cracked, and even burned pigment caused by a hot light bulb. Fluorescent light, while cool in temperature, has an even greater capacity to fade sensitive objects. Special fluorescent bulbs or protective sleeves which prevent the escape of damaging ultra-violet light are available for cautious collectors.

The occasional rotation of objects in a collection, or changing their placement from time to time, is also an effective way to reduce damage caused over a long period by even relatively low light levels.

The damaging effect of the prolonged exposure of a textile
to sunlight can be seen by comparing it with the unfaded
shape left by the antimacassar which protected it.
American platform rocker (c. 1880) with sun-faded
upholstery. (Photo: Jim Barbour)

Rugs may be turned seasonally to prevent fading, or even traffic wear at one end, and furniture near windows can be alternated with other pieces which have not been sitting in light. It is not only soft, absorbent materials which are affected by the action of light, since both glass and glazed ceramics may also be damaged by it. While sunlight fades color from textiles, it *gives* color to glass. Depending on the metallic impurities that much glass contains, strong light, even over a relatively short time span, can cause clear glass to take on a blue, green, purple, or yellow tinge. This change is irreversible. The glaze on ceramics, which is of a different physical and chemical character than the clay it covers, may become crackled over time as the exposure to heat and light causes an expansion and contraction of the two materials at different rates.

Dirt

Impurities in the air of the industrialized world, amply described in every environmental report, hold chemicals, dirt, spores, toxins, and corrosives in such quantity that it is amazing that all antiques and collectors alike have not been consumed or buried by them. These agents have imperiled monuments from the Parthenon in Athens and Gothic sculpture in France to practically everything in Venice and Pittsburgh. The average homeowners or collectors can do only so much to protect their property from these effects, insidious as they may be. Many antiques and collectibles, of course, need virtually no care. Glass, ceramics, and most metal and wooden objects are preserved best when the least is done to them, and it might well be argued that more antiques have been damaged from overzealous cleaning and "restoration" than from the natural accumulation of dirt. Providing a reasonable environment and a normal amount of general housekeeping may be all that is necessary for their protection. There are, however, a few kinds of antiques for which a modest understanding of some simple conservation procedures will insure their longevity.

The removal of surface dirt as it occurs is the most practical approach to keeping collections in good condition. Dusting with a clean, soft cloth is the only regular attention that most antiques need. Invisible as it may be, the same amount of dust which is falling on a polished mahogany dining table is also falling on carpets and upholstery. When it comes in contact with damp bodies and damp air, this dirt causes upholstery to soil and discolor. Normal vacuuming prevents much of the problem. Small Oriental rugs may be gently shaken of their dirt by grasping them firmly on their side, but not snapped on end, since this can cause old rugs to unravel or even split. Larger rugs should be vacuumed regularly to remove sand, which cuts fibers. Tank-type cleaners are better than uprights which have a beating action and tend to cause abrasion and actually remove rug fibers along with the soil.

More mythology has been created regarding the care of wooden furniture than any other medium to which collectors might direct their attention. Contrary to the firmly held notions of many, furniture does not need any regular special attention in order to assure its proper conservation. A lot of money has been made by purveyors of products who intensify the guilt of collectors who imagine they should be "doing something" for their furniture. Wood does not need to be "fed." Treatments made for this spurious purpose are almost always oily (tung, linseed, or lemon oil); they only momentarily make the surface look slicker, and they attract dust and eventually darken the surface. Regularly removing dirt by dusting with a slightly damp cloth *with* the grain of furniture is the surest way to avoid having the dust act as an abrasive. Commercial sprays for polishing or dusting, which are directly applied to the furniture, should be avoided entirely, though their occasional use, first applied to a cloth, may be more acceptable. On a regular basis they are unnecessary, and they may leave a deposit which eventually builds up to discolor the wood. If wood really needs any protection at all, it is best accomplished by applying a thin layer of good commercial paste wax once a year and buffing with a soft cloth.

The washing of antique textiles should be done with the greatest care and the most conservative application of foreign substances. Before washing, it is always important to consider whether the presence and appearance of dirt are more harmful to the preservation and enjoyment of the item than the cleaning itself would be. Cotton, wool, and linen may be safely washed if the fabric is dimensionally stable, not brittle or unravelled, and has been tested to see if the colors are fast. Hand-washing with a ph-balanced soap such as Orvis, or any nondetergent soap, followed by many deep rinses to remove all traces of the cleaner, is the most satisfactory method of removing soil. Soaps, whose residue is left in a textile, will yellow the material, and may do even greater harm than dirt over time. While even professional cleaning of rugs causes the loss of some lanolin from the wool fibers, dirt, especially that which is ground in, is even more immediately perilous. Dry cleaning of old textiles should generally be avoided unless it is done by hand, without the usual tumbling and spinning which may damage old fibers.

Assuming first that anyone should have a collection so large that it cannot all be seen, but parts of it must be stored somewhere out of view, the proper storage of old textiles is a simple matter when a few general procedures are followed. First, flat textiles such as coverlets, quilts, and handwork pieces are best stored clean and *unironed*. Second, their storage should be in containers that will prevent dust from entering and which will isolate the textiles from harmful substances. The ever popular cedar chest, for example, in which generations of

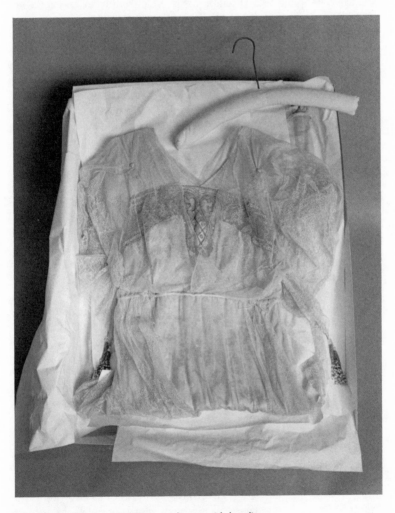

Historic garments too fragile or too heavy with beading to be hung on padded hangers should be padded with acid-free paper to prevent harsh folds and placed in acid-free boxes. Silk and lace beaded and embroidered evening gown (c. 1914). Hennepin County Historical Society, Minneapolis. (Photo: Jim Barbour)

wedding dresses and baby clothes have traditionally been stored, is a very poor place to save almost anything. Wood, and cedar in particular, along with many other everyday materials, such as cardboard, paper and polyethylene, contain resins and acids, and emit gases that can actually deteriorate and discolor items which come in contact with them. This is also true of mothballs, insect repellent flakes, and sprays which are sold commercially and placed directly or indirectly on or near the textiles. Items placed in wooden or cardboard containers, including the drawers of furniture, should be isolated from the wood with clear Mylar (available from any art supply store), and each textile should be wrapped loosely with *acid-free* tissue paper. The blue gift-wrap tissue used by so many in the past for this purpose is *not* an acceptable substitute. Large acid-free suit boxes and tissue may be purchased by mail through museum supply companies. Third, textiles should be stored so that a minimum amount of folding is required. Harsh, crisp folds may form permanent creases in the structure of fabrics when stored for long periods, especially if the weight of others is on them. Acid-free boxes of sufficient size to minimize the number of folds are ideal. The few folds, then, should be gentle ones, each padded with a wadding of proper tissue or washed, unbleached muslin along their length. To avoid stress on the textile of which they are composed, historic costumes, if they are weighty with beads or other embellishments, should also be laid in boxes. Other garments are best placed on padded hangers to distribute their weight at the shoulders. Ordinary wire hangers may rust, wooden hangers are not chemically neutral, and neither provide proper support. To keep their form, old hats and shoes should be stuffed with acid-free tissue.

The Enemy Within

One of the misfortunes of earlier technology (and who knows about contemporary technology?) is that certain materials, in and of themselves, deteriorate and destroy the items whose structures they form. In the museum world this phenomenon is known by the sinister term, *inherent vice*. Such is the case with certain kinds of silk and paper and varnish.

Every collector has seen parasols whose silk coverings are shredded, crazy quilts where all the black pieces are almost gone, or Victorian wedding dresses that fall apart when they are touched. In the nineteenth century, silk was treated with metallic salts to give it weight and "rustle." Consequently, these materials are called "weighted silks." The presence of these reagents in the silk, through time, eventually causes the material to deteriorate entirely. While there is absolutely

"Inherent vice" refers to potentially destructive materials
within an object. Weighted silks are one such example,
and will deteriorate irreversibly over time. Detail of a
quilt deteriorating because of the metallic salts within the
silk itself. (Photo: Jim Barbour)

nothing that current technology can do to reverse or even stop this process, collectors should be reminded that it is best, when buying, to check for damage already started.

Paper is the second common material that presents conservation problems for the collector. Before the mid-nineteenth century, almost all paper was made of natural materials, fibers of cotton and linen rags, without the intervention of harmful ingredients that made them unstable. Thus, even ancient papers have survived remarkably intact. However, around the time of the Civil War, wood pulp with its high lignin content and the use of acidic products to process paper were introduced. By 1900 the practice had become widespread, as newsprint and other commercial paper products were almost always made this way. The acidic composition of these materials made the papers photoreactive and caused them in a few brief years to become yellowed, brown, and brittle. For those who collect maps, drawings, letters, greeting cards, photographs, and other documents that are made of such paper, a realistic view of their potential inherent hazards is the best defense in the prevention of others. Brown spots, often found on old paper, are called *foxing* and are probably caused by fungi and iron salts in the paper. No one but a professional paper conservator should attempt to remove such discoloration.

The action of light on unstable papers hastens their deterioration through fading and other chemical changes. Paper goods should therefore be stored or displayed away from windows and fluorescent light sources. Paper of any kind should be isolated from acidic materials including other papers. Any collector who has ever opened up a picture under glass is aware of how responsive paper is to the action of materials adjacent to it. Prints unprotected from the backing boards of a picture frame will take on the pattern of their wood grain from the gradual oozing of its acids and resins. Likewise, *mat-burn* can be seen when a picture on paper is separated from its enframing mat, revealing a brown rectangle that has been burned into the art work because of contact with an acid-based mat board. Prints and drawings under glass should always be protected with matting and backing made of acid-free paper or board. The mat board also provides the art with air space essential to its proper care.

Original art should never be placed directly next to glass, as changes of atmospheric conditions may cause paint or ink pigments, and certainly pastel or chalk, to stick to it. Framing with Plexiglas should be avoided if the art is either charcoal or chalk. Plexiglas has the capacity for attracting static electricity, and may draw particles of the medium from the paper to its own surface. The use of any pressure-sensitive tape, such as adhesive, cellophane, or masking tape, to affix pictures to mats is an absolute taboo. All have oils that eventually seep into the paper and cause discoloration that may spread even beyond their point of contact. Art on paper should be suspended from its backing support by acid-free linen hinges placed at the top of the picture, so

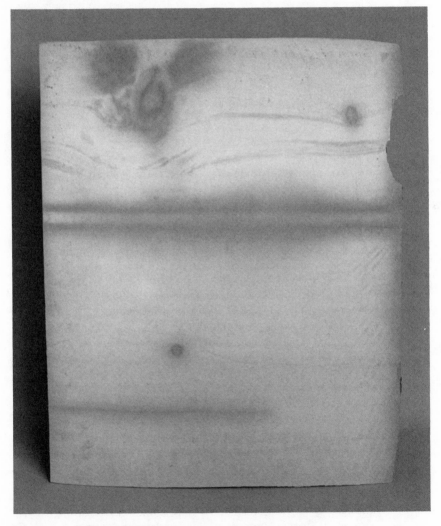

The reverse side of a framed print, backed by a piece of wood, is damaged by the acids oozing from it, creating a permanent pattern of its grain and knots. (Photo: Jim Barbour)

that the art work hangs freely along the sides and bottom to prevent puckering. Pictures under glass should also have a dust shield of paper glued tautly to the back of the frame.

The varnishes which have been traditionally used as protection on old paintings and furniture are another kind of substance that contains the cause of its own discoloration. Varnishes, particularly those used throughout the nineteenth century, often contained bitumen, an asphalt-like material used as a binder. Through exposure to heat, light, and through its own internal changes, bitumen may cause checked or alligatored surfaces, which, short of refinishing, are not easily disguised.

The Moving of Antiques

The potential for immediate and massive damage to antiques is never closer at hand than when single items or whole households are moved from place to place. Taking a veneered desk from a heated shop into an ice-cold van in midwinter can be traumatic to both its wood and glue. Likewise, objects stored in some breezy barn and brought into a heated interior can be affected just as adversely by rapid changes of temperature and humidity. Cut glass, ivory, and jade, too, have been known to split from sudden and dramatic heat or moisture loss.

Furniture, when moved even within the house, should always be lifted, never dragged. Dragging furniture across a room can loosen and even break off legs, and causes undue stress to all joints. The use of professional movers is no guarantee that maximum protection will be given to antiques. Moving crews faced with anything more subtle than the usual sofa bed or pool table, and unfamiliar with its care, will occasionally act with unthinkable carelessness toward the artifacts entrusted to them. Any collector faced with such a prospect would do well to shout periodic warnings to the movers and be constantly vigilant while trucks and containers are being packed. Insurance adjusters are kept quite busy investigating claims of damage caused to items packed and moved by professionals. Even the slight movements of cargo are enough to cause great damage to goods if the packing is not properly done. A few boxes of books or records atop a delicate table can reduce it to splinters within a few hundred miles of subtle shifting in the truck's load. The ample use of padding between furniture to prevent abrasion and nesting things comfortably without stress are good protection against major structural damage or surface marring.

Many people who move their collections prefer to pack the smaller items themselves. This is certainly the best way to insure their proper care. But most professional movers will not insure such loads unless their own crew has done the packing. This problem is easily solved by the homeowners taking out a short-term rider on their regular household insurance policy if it is not already included. The important thing to remember when packing small items is to prevent their damage from the exterior, and from other objects in the same container. A heavy flat iron and a porcelain cup should never be packed together no matter how much padding there is between them. Boxes from the grocery or liquor store, which have compartmentalized inserts, are the most satisfactory containers for glassware and related items.

The use of newspapers for padding, though popular and cheap, is best avoided because of the smeary ink they contain which, even if it is not in direct contact with the antique, gets all over the hands of the packer and is transferred to everything in sight. Do-it-yourself moving companies sell quantities of plain newsprint paper cheaply. Using this uninked paper saves the washing of every piece of china and stemware before it is put away again.

Safety

Every collector (and certainly every dealer) has a couple of horror stories about accidents which have taken their antiques from them. They run the gamut from the delivery truck which backed up into the stall of art glass at a major antique show to the more focussed damage caused by a flying champagne cork. Pets, kids, shaky relatives, or drunken friends aside, anyone who has antiques is bound to have some loss through normal usage. A few simple precautions reduce the chances of disaster.

Even antiquities not classified as "breakable" are, nevertheless, subject to some danger of damage, as has been noted previously. Even the collector of cast-iron stoves may worry about dropping and cracking one during a move. One of the most common breaches of good sense among collectors of fragile objects is to place them in locked what-not cabinets with shelves made of window glass. Glass, particularly if it is old and has been used horizontally to support even minimal weight over many years, eventually becomes stressed and brittle. Quite spontaneously old shelves may give way like the St. Andreas fault, and the ensuing cascade of shards and *objets d'art* will destroy everything displayed beneath it. Unless shelves are made of thick plate glass or heavy Plexiglas, they represent a disaster waiting to happen.

Three-legged tables are unorthodox and, no matter how beautiful, are tippy, and should never be adorned with anything which cannot afford a fall on the floor because some child or clumsy adult has put the piece off balance. Objects placed on shelves have a tendency to slowly "creep" because of vibrations caused by foot traffic in the house or by road traffic outside. A slight beaded edging on open shelves is usually enough to stop such movement. Pictures should always be affixed to the wall with heavy, braided picture wire on two picture hooks of generous size. This measure not only provides greater safety for the picture, but prevents the continual releveling of it dangling from a single point. The household condition most easily controlled for the safety of collections is that of density of display. Like overcrowded antique shops, private houses filled to the ceiling with every manner of object are not only poor showcases in which to really see and appreciate items of quality, but they are uncomfortable places for visitors and pose a danger to everything in them.

Security

The best security for any collection is to have the lowest possible visibility and access by anyone who might do it harm. However, because antiques were meant to be seen, used, and enjoyed, a certain amount of exposure to potential damage and theft is simply a fact of normal living. There are many paintings just as great, wonderful, and valuable as Rembrandt's *Night Watch* or Leonardo's Mona Lisa; yet, one has been the victim of vandals and the other of thieves on several occasions. But because these masterpieces are perennially in the media and are thus so well known, they quite naturally (despite the obsessive security measures lavished on them) have become the targets for extortionists and crazies, who can be assured of attention by placing them in peril. Collections of early pressed glass kept in vaults do not get broken, and private caches of gold coins not known to thieves are safe. But collectors quite naturally want to enjoy their possessions with use and wish others to see and admire them.

The visibility of collections from the exterior of a house is the surest invitation to trouble. Glass collectors are notorious for displaying their wares in windows where the light is flattering (if damaging) to them. Tiffany lamps which can be seen from the street also attract unwanted attention. With the regular media attention given to antiques, collectors can no longer depend upon the ignorance of the "average thief" regarding the value of antiques, and, therefore, should maintain as anonymous a facade as is possible. The stereotypical use by many antique buffs of outdoor decorations such as wagon wheels, American eagles, cute colonial mailboxes, iron jockeys, and sleighs planted with geraniums simply advertise that antique collectors (if tasteless ones) reside within. Window treatments which prevent exterior inventories from passers-by, as well as exterior lighting, are also effective and cheap insurance.

The installation of security systems, unfortunately a sign of the times, is now being practiced by many homeowners whether or not they collect antiques. To many, the use of such protection appears overreactive and unnecessary; some maintain that the mere presence of such a system is an advertisement to would-be thieves that there is something inside worth taking. The cost of several thousand dollars for a professionally installed system may seem excessive. Yet the loss of a single rug, picture, or clock could easily amount to that much. Less expensive alarm systems may give a false sense of security and end up costing plenty because they are not reliable. Security systems do not necessarily prevent trouble, and in themselves may be problematic. Almost any alarm system will occasionally be set off accidentally, and noisy alarms mounted on the exterior of houses are an annoyance to neighbors who, if regularly disturbed by them, may ignore a true emergency when it arises. Signals that directly alert the security company sometimes bring the quickest response to trouble, but they usually cost more because of the personnel involved.

Fire in anyone's home is fearful to contemplate, and for collectors it is horrifying. Good housekeeping and good sense is the best prevention. Sensibly, many municipalities now require apartments and single-family houses to be equipped with smoke detectors which protect both occupants and collections. House fires have been known to ignite from the action of sunlight through the window, intensified to a flash point by passing through a cut-glass vase or a kerosene lamp displayed before it.

Inventories

The proper management of any collection, whether in a museum or in private hands, requires an inventory. The prudent addition to or subtraction from a collection necessitates a thorough knowledge of its contents. Many collectors, of course, have this inventory in their heads, and their information is often remarkably complete and accurate as to what they have, what it is worth, and where they got it. For some collectors a mental accounting is all that is necessary. These same people who have prepared for life's every inevitable event by owning household, health and life insurance, and even a cemetery lot, however, overlook the potential for chaos while their precious possessions remain uncataloged. Many a surviving family member has been short-changed both intellectually and financially by inheriting the task of disposing of a collection they neither understood nor knew the value of.

While inventories are necessary for insurance, they may also be a pleasant exercise in the regular re-evaluation of one's collection. The simple act of writing down the data for a single object and, eventually, the accumulation of information on the entire collection, assists the collector in seeing direction, growth, strengths, and gaps which need filling. A useful inventory will include the name of the object and suffi-cient description to differentiate it from others of its kind including size, color, and other identifying characteristics, as well as the date and loca-tion of purchase and its cost. Other data worth noting may include remarks about its history, who owned it, and a pencilled-in notation of its current market value which can be regularly updated.

Written inventories may be supplemented with photographs of objects, or even supplanted by them. The easiest inventory system to create is accomplished by photographing every wall of every room and the contents of drawers and closets. Some entrepreneurs provide cus-tom-made video taped inventories for collectors. Certain kinds of col-lections, such as coins, medals, carved gems, and other small items, require high-quality photographs for their documentation and to assist collectors in their study of details.

Insurance

Some insurance agents, used to writing policies on snowmobiles, new cars, boats, and general household goods, get nervous when asked to supply coverage for antiques. When choosing an underwriter it is best to find one who is familiar with insuring antiques and art and is used to scheduled property matters. The best way to find a good insur-ance company and agent is to ask other collector friends whom they use, particularly if they have ever made a claim. All insurance compa-nies willingly accept annual premiums, though many fewer are as eager to pay settlements with a minimum of fuss, particularly for objects whose value they cannot look up in a price book. Calling local mu-seums to find out who carries their policy is often a good clue to an agency's sophistication in specialized insurance matters relative to col-lectibles.

Having an insurance policy which is appropriate to a collector's needs requires some preliminary effort on the part of the policyholder. A complete inventory is a prerequisite and is, in any event, essential to the good management of any collection. While most insurance policies cover general household goods, it is best when insuring antiques to have a *scheduled* policy. This is simply a listing of each important item with its value. Some companies insist upon a written outside appraisal for these objects, others accept the owner's evaluations based on re-placement costs. It is wise to update the schedule annually, adding new acquisitions and removing disposed of goods. Evaluations should also be updated to agree with current market prices. It is often surprising how little a few thousand dollars of extra coverage actually costs in terms of the premium paid.

8

THE MISUSE OF ANTIQUES

Joanne had always considered herself artistic
and the trait was beginning to show itself again
like the dark roots of her hair. She took the
coffee grinder off the shelf where it had been
sitting since the divorce, knowing now it was
safe to wire it up for a lamp.

Florence Vincent
The Unpleasantness on Grove Street

The people who are the most admiring of old things are often the same ones responsible for their disrespectful alteration or their destruction. Most obvious is the case of scroungers who "liberate" architectural elements, stained glass, and the like from old buildings; it is a characteristic no less true of a few antique collectors. Old Wilcox and Gibbs or Singer sewing machines with cast-iron frames and oak drawers are regularly cannibalized by their owners by removing mechanical parts and making the stands into tables and drawers into "memorabilia boxes." Every collector should consciously avoid the inappropriate cleverness which this kind of misuse represents.

Horrifying as it seems, some antique collectors, anxious to customize antique pieces for their own needs will destroy perfectly fine furniture by shortening the legs of tables to match the height of their sofa, or reduce the length of bed posts to fit a cramped attic space. With the greatest regularity, engraved and lithographed illustrations are excised from intact historic folio volumes by dealers and collectors alike looking for decorative art suitable for framing.

Some antiques can be misused without altering them in any way, simply because they are placed in illogical settings or put to irrational uses. No matter how magnificent its design or construction, a cobbler's bench is still just that. It does not belong before a sofa to be used as a coffee table. Nor does a dry sink—a necessary evil at best—belong in a dining room, filled with philodendrons. And no self-respecting farmer would have allowed a cream can to be placed as a conversation piece in his parlor or even in his kitchen, even if it were decoupaged with old sheet music! Two-man pit saws were never meant to be displayed inside a house, and when used this way as decoration, only appear menacing to those seated beneath them. For that matter, spinning wheels—the enduring symbol of the antique collector—were not generally used in parlors unless they were one-room log houses. Chamber pots used as planters or even as tureens on the tabletop are certain to turn a diner off the soup course.

Antiques may be abused in innumerable ways through ignorance, neglect, or careless usage. But there is also another form of misuse, perhaps more subtle, to which collectors should be alerted lest they fall into its trap. The enlightened collector of fine period furniture, or the sophisticated specialist of Chinese porcelain, is unlikely to be affected by it. It is rather the beginning collectors of general-line merchandise, particularly those who are fond of country things and "primitives," who seem to be the most prone to practice a particular kind of misuse with disturbing abandon.

This misuse happens innocently enough as many of the purposes for which objects now regarded as antiques were made are no longer practiced. Thus candle molds, butter churns, coffee grinders, oiling cans, and cream cans, whose original functions are now passé but whose charms and curiosities are recognized and appreciated, are all too often transformed into lamps by the well-meaning scrounger. Motivated by a desire to have everything in a decorating scheme look old, even if its function is modern, collectors will sometimes turn wagon wheels and old brass fire extinguishers into lighting fixtures, brass and iron beds into settees. This is, of course, a travesty to the character and intention of the antique, as well as an illogical and inefficient approach to lighting design.

Since the advent of electric light, the designing of lamps from elements of alien artifacts has provided a free-for-all for bad taste. Apparently embarrassed by an honestly simple and functional solution to a twentieth-century problem, collectors have regularly drilled holes into Staffordshire dogs, Ch'ing Dynasty ginger jars, and Meissen figurines to which they then attach sockets, wires, and fringed shades. A somewhat more acceptable adaptation for old lighting, but nevertheless still damaging to the original character of the object, is the electrification of kerosene, oil, or gas lamps. This transformation can be accomplished without damage to the original lamp through the replacement of burners (which should be saved) with electric sockets. The current fashion for stripping the nickel plating from kerosene lamp bases to reveal the brass beneath, however, should be discouraged.

Iron, copper, and brass kettles and other containers are regularly

The popular misuses of antiques often include embellishment with inappropriate applied decorations or forcing them to serve functions for which they were never intended. Tin candle mold (c. 1870) made into a lamp; decorated flatiron. Anonymous collection. (Photo: Jim Barbour)

used quite thoughtlessly by collectors for planters, often directly filled with dirt. The sturdiest iron pot can be reduced to a pile of rust in a few short years from the dampness of the soil in it, and copper and brass vessels corrode even more quickly. Textiles such as coverlets and quilts are sometimes casually used for tablecloths or even draperies—a function for which they were never intended. They are much more fragile than linen and not as easily cleaned. It is well for the collector to remember to use antiques in a manner (and in a place) consistent with their original intention, or as a reasonable extension of it.

9

LIVING WITH A COLLECTION

As home is the place where our best and
happiest hours are passed, nothing which will
beautify or adorn it can be of trifling importance.

Sarah Josepha Hale
*Manners; or, Happy Homes and Good
Society All the Year Round*

The objects whose utility, beauty, and quality have caused people to collect and save them were created first to be used and enjoyed. Most were not meant to be put in locked drawers, behind bullet-proof glass, or in vaults. Along with the thrill of their discovery, *living* with antiques is the greatest pleasure they give; they should be a source of joy to their owners, and not an encumbrance. This fact does not prevent some collectors from being so consumed by the preciousness of their possessions that paranoia controls their lives. No collector is more pathetic than the one who refuses entrance to workmen, or hospitality to visitors, for fear they will discover what treasures they own and thus imperil their security. Likewise, there are those who keep their silver, great pictures, or grandfather's watch collection in a bank vault. They might better sell such property to those who will enjoy it, or give it to a museum where an appreciative public will be enriched. Antiques which are inaccessible by being stuffed in drawers, closets, and attics where they are never seen are antiques which are not enjoyed — except when the estate sale is conducted.

The thoughtful accumulation of antiques is accomplished by a preliminary evaluation of the potential utility and satisfaction derived from each object in it. Antiques which are used frequently provide the greatest pleasure. Utilitarian pieces need to function: beds and chairs should be comfortable, tables should be stable and sturdy, and drawers should move with minimum effort. Even museums avoid acquiring antiquities which are too delicate or fragile for exhibition. Objects whose fragility or requirements of very special care preclude their use in a normal household setting should not be purchased in the first place. Even the most cautious collectors have to accept the fact that accidents will occasionally cause damage to antiques. Very few antiques are sacred, and the ones which are probably do not belong in private hands.

Few antiques ever just "wear out" from normal everyday use. A Queen Anne highboy might easily have served multiple generations of the family in which it descended with no substantial change in its integrity or condition. The fact that, even in continuous use, an Oriental rug can last several hundred years is evidence enough that such textiles can be more durable than modern nylon carpeting. Even children and antiques can be compatible, and the presence of collections in a household does not automatically necessitate a curtailing of an active family life. The beauty of antiques—the major reason for possessing them in the first place—is the source of visual enrichment for all who are willing to learn the game, exercise the judgment, and spend the time and money to acquire them.

Antiques provide an enriching environment in which to live. The process of acquiring a collection is an activity in which every family member might take an interest. Harry and Morgan Sheff and friend at home with antiques. (Photo: Harold and Virginia Sheff)

GLOSSARY

Absentee bid

A bid given by the customer in writing to the auction house prior to the sale and presented on their behalf by the house's commission bidder during the sale. Absentee bidding is a service provided by most auction houses for customers not wanting to sit through an entire sale or who may wish to remain anonymous. Absentee bids are legally binding.

Acid-free

A condition of paper, cloth, plastic, or other material that guarantees it to have a neutral Ph balance of around 7. Being neither acid nor alkaline, it will not emit harmful fumes that might discolor or speed the deterioration of artifacts placed in contact with them.

Antique

Originally a term specifically referring to the ancient world, and later only to those items which were hand made, but now generally accepted as embracing those objects of quality and often beauty in excess of one hundred years old.

Antique show

A temporary exhibition of antiques offered for sale by many dealers collectively. These sales occur with regularity in most larger cities and offer the collector merchandise from across the country, often of great variety and depth as well as a consistency of quality.

Antique supermarket/mall

A cooperative system in which antique dealers sell their merchandise under one roof while sharing expenses of rent, utilities, insurance, and advertising.

Appraisal

An oral or written statement about the identity and value of an object. The utility of an appraisal is dependent upon the integrity and expertise of the person giving it, and the purpose for which it was intended. Appraisals are often intended to establish value for insurance or tax purposes and should not necessarily be construed to mean the sale value of an antique.

Assembled set

A grouping of various pieces of porcelain, silver, or glass not originally made together that have been matched up at some later date to comprise a complete service.

Auction

A periodically held public sale of property sold to the highest bidder by agents who act on behalf of the owners for a commission. Auctions may be conducted by international or local auction houses, rural auctioneers, traveling auction galleries, or even by mail.

Bid

An offer by an auction customer to buy a lot at a certain price. The auctioneer solicits and accepts increasingly higher competing bids and is the final determiner of the highest or winning bid. Bids are agreements by the bidder to meet the auctioneer's request and are proffered by raising a hand, a card, a paddle, or one's voice.

Buyer's premium

A percentage of the hammer price (usually 10%) added to the buyer's final bid that together comprise the actual purchase price of lots bought at auction.

Buy-in

An action exercised by the commission bidder at an auction house to retrieve lots for the seller that have not achieved their established reserve. Buy-ins cost the consignor money, usually a percentage of the reserve price.

Cleanup

The residue from an estate sale comprised of all the unsold merchandise including both undesirable items or those that were priced too high. Individuals engaged in selling used goods will often buy a cleanup, the entire remaining contents, for a modest amount of cash.

Collectible

Any object deemed worthy of collecting which cannot be accurately classified as an antique by virtue of its being newer or, possibly, less important. With time and re-evaluation, collectibles may become antiques.

Collection

A conscious selection and organization of similar or related objects to form a unified whole. A collection has direction and may have as its focus a style, historical period, material or medium, or the type or function of an object.

Commission

A charge to the owner of property established by the auction house for their service of selling it. Commission is often based on a sliding scale, a percentage of the actual selling price of the consigned merchandise.

Commission bidder

An agent of an auction house, acting on behalf of the consignor of property who insures that if a lot does not achieve the reserve figure, it is bought-in by the house to be returned to the owner.

Consignment

Any property which is entrusted to a seller, usually an auctioneer or antique dealer. Consignors are paid only upon the sale of the property and are charged a percentage of the sale price by the consignee, usually ranging from five to thirty-five percent.

Design

The appearance of an object created by the arrangements of its parts and details to produce a unified whole. The quality of design is the overwhelmingly important factor in establishing the value of an antique.

Divvie

(see picker)

Estate

The entire property of an individual whether living or dead.

Estate sale

A marketing event, usually conducted from a private residence, in which the entire unedited contents of a home are offered for sale including antiques, books, clothing, appliances, and miscellaneous housewares.

Estimate

The approximate price, established by the auction house, that a lot is predicted to bring. Estimates are usually published in advance and are expressed as a double number, including a low and high figure to represent the possible range of bidding.

Expert

A person who, by virtue of his or her position, experience, or education, knows more about the authenticity, history, and value of an antique than the individual asking his or her advice.

Expertise clinic

An educational service often sponsored by a museum, educational institution, or major auction house that provides a panel of authorities who will identify and sometimes evaluate the property the general public brings to them.

Flea market

Informal, temporary settings for the selling of antiques, collectibles, and general merchandise, promoted and run by people who own, rent, or manage the property on which they are held. They sometimes are referred to as swap meets. Sellers at flea markets may be amateurs or professionals who usually expect to bargain with customers.

Foxing

The discoloration found on old paper, usually in the form of brown spots, caused by fungi or iron salts in the paper. Foxing can be successfully removed and prevented only by a professional conservator.

Garage sale

An informal periodic event conducted by homeowners singly or in groups for the disposal of unwanted household goods. These amateur events may also be called yard sales or tag sales and, if combined with others in a neighborhood, block sales.

General-line shop

An antique store that does not pursue a specialty but rather offers a broad variety of general merchandise including antique furniture, accessories, glassware, china, paper goods, and other collectibles.

Hammer price

The last and winning bid in an auction marked by the fall of the auctioneer's hammer. This is different than the actual purchase price, which is the total of the hammer price and the buyer's premium.

Inherent vice

Material within an object that acts to deteriorate and destroy the structure itself. Certain kinds of paper and silk often contain these agents. The action of inherent vice is generally irreversible.

Investment

Expenditure for the purpose of obtaining income or profit. Successful investment in antiques requires the expertise that allows buying at wholesale and selling at retail within a reasonable period of time.

Mail order

A system for buying antiques, sight unseen, through the mail. Many dealers exclusively conduct this kind of business in which their goods are described in journal advertisements or in catalogs that they publish and send to customers.

Marriage

The act of making a complete object from parts of several others, most often seen in furniture. A married highboy, for example, would consist of the top and bottom of two originally unrelated, though compatible, pieces.

Patina

The surface quality of objects caused by age, use, oxidation, and exposure to environmental impurities. Patination on antiques of many materials occurs naturally over time as a color change or a thin coat of minute scratches. A rich, deep patina may be a good measure of age and is considered highly desirable in period furniture.

Picker
A dealer in antiques who acts as an independent buying and selling agent to a loosely defined group of customers, most of whom are other dealers. Pickers do not have shops and hold very little inventory. Also known as runners, divvies, scouts and barkers.

Plant
An anonymous agent for an auction house who poses as an audience bidder to buy back merchandise owned by the house which does not achieve a profitable margin from its wholesale purchase price. Also known as stooges or shills.

Planting
The act of adding merchandise from other sources to an estate sale in order to increase its volume or quality. Also known as seeding.

Preview
The presale exhibition period of lots to be auctioned available for examination by any interested parties, usually several days prior to the sale.

Provenance
The origin or source of an object. A complete provenance is the history of the ownership of an object from the time of its creation. When known by the vendor, provenance may have considerable effect on the price of an antique.

Reserve
A limit figure given by the consignor of goods below which he or she is not willing to sell the lot. The reserve, agreed upon jointly by the consignor and the house, protects the consignor, particularly of expensive property, from heavy losses due to an indifferent market.

Runner
(see picker)

Salers
Those persons who periodically or habitually pursue antiques and collectibles by attending garage, yard, and estate sales.

Scheduled property
Those items specifically enumerated on insurance policies that are individually evaluated. In the event of loss, the insurance agent generally pays the policy holder the full amount of their appraised value.

Shelf piece
A euphemism used to describe antiques and collectibles that are in less than perfect condition, but for some collectors look acceptable on a shelf or in a curio cabinet.

Shill
(see plant)

Stooge
(see plant)

Style
A manner of treatment or execution of an object that gives it its geographical or chronological identity. Style is caused by a combination of specific features including its ornament, proportion, and material.

Swap meets
(see flea markets)

Tag sale
(see garage sale)

Telephone bid
An offer by an auction customer who is not in attendance at the sale to buy a lot by telephone. Telephone bids are treated as though the buyer were there and are immediately relayed by an agent of the house to the bidding floor.

Ultraviolet
Certain light rays of extremely short

wave length just beyond the violet end of the visible spectrum. Both sunlight and fluorescent lamps emit ultraviolet waves that are exceedingly damaging to the stability of the color and material integrity of antiquities. Especially vulnerable to these rays are paper, cloth, and wood, though even glass can be altered by them.

Yard sale
(see garage sale)

SELECTED
BIBLIOGRAPHY

Basic Collecting

Battersby, Martin. *The Decorative Thirties.* New York: Walker and Company, 1971. 208 pp., illus., bibliog.

Battersby, Martin. *The Decorative Twenties.* New York: Walker and Company, 1969. 216 pp., illus., bibliog.

Butler, Joseph T. *American Antiques 1800–1900: A Collector's History and Guide.* New York: Odyssey Press, 1965. 203 pp., illus., bibliog.

Comstock, Helen. *The Concise Encyclopedia of American Antiques.* New York: Hawthorn Books, 1969. 848 pp., illus., bibliog.

Hammond, Dorothy. *Confusing Collectibles: A Guide to the Identification of Reproductions.* Leon, la.: Mid-American Book Co., 1969–1972. 2 vols., illus., bibliog.

Hillier, Bevis. *The Decorative Arts of the Forties and Fifties: Austerity/Binge.* New York: Clarkson N. Potter, Inc., 1975. 200 pp., illus.

Israel, Fred L., ed. *1897 Sears Roebuck Catalogue.* New York: Chelsea House Publishers, 1968. 786 pp., index.

Kelley, Austin P., and Sotheby Parke Bernet Staff. *Anatomy of Antiques: A Collector's Guide.* New York: Viking Press, 1974. 189 pp., illus.

Kirk, John. *The Impecunious Collector's Guide to American Antiques.* New York: Alfred A. Knopf, 1975. 174 pp., illus.

Kovel, Ralph M., and Terry J. Kovel. *The Complete Antiques Price List: A Guide to the Market for Professionals, Dealers, and Collectors.* New York: Crown Publications, 1969–present. 1 vol. annually, illus.

MacDonald-Taylor, Margaret. *A Dictionary of Marks: Metalwork, Furniture, Ceramics; The Identification Handbook for Antique Collectors.* New York: Hawthorn Books, Inc., 1962. 318 pp., illus., bibliog.

MacLeish, A. Bruce. *The Care of Antiques and Historical Collections.* Nashville, Tenn.: The American Association of State and Local History Press, 1972, 1986. 248 pp., list of suppliers for conservation materials and equipment.

Osborne, Harold, ed. *The Oxford Companion to the Decorative Arts.* Oxford, England: Clarendon Press, 1975. 865 pp., illus., bibliog.

Peterson, Harold L. *How Do You Know It's Old? A Practical Handbook on the Detection of Fakes for the Antique Collector and Curator.* New York: Charles Scribner's Sons, 1975. 166 pp., illus., bibliog.

Random House. *The Random House Collector's Encyclopedia: Victorian to Art Deco*. New York: Random House, 1974. 303 pp., illus., bibliog.

Rinker, Harry L., ed. *Warman's Antiques and Their Prices*. Elkins Park, Pa.: Warman Publishing Co., Inc., 1949–present. 1 vol. annually, illus.

Romaine, Lawrence B. *A Guide to American Trade Catalogs 1744–1900*. New York: R. R. Bowker Co., 1960. 422 pp.

Savage, George. *Dictionary of Antiques*. New York: Frederick A. Praeger, 1970. 534 pp., illus., bibliog.

Yates, Raymond F. *Antique Fakes and Their Detection*. New York: Award Books, 1972. 229 pp., illus.

Ceramics

Chaffers, William. *Collector's Handbook of Marks and Monograms on Pottery and Porcelain*. 4th ed. London: W. Reeves, 1968. 367 pp., illus.

Charleston, Robert J. *World Ceramics: An Illustrated History*. New York: McGraw-Hill, 1968. 352 pp., illus., bibliog.

Cox, Warren Earle. *The Book of Pottery and Porcelain*. New York: Crown Publishers, 1970. 2 vols., 1,158 pp., illus.

Godden, Geoffrey A. *The Handbook of British Pottery and Porcelain Marks*. New York: Frederick A. Praeger, 1968. 197 pp., illus., bibliog.

Godden, Geoffrey A. *An Illustrated Encyclopedia of British Pottery and Porcelain*. New York: Bonanza Books, 1965. 390 pp., illus., bibliog.

Hillier, Bevis. *Pottery and Porcelain, 1700–1914: England, Europe and North America*. New York: Meredith Press, 1968. 386 pp., illus., bibliog.

Kovel, Ralph M., and Terry J. Kovel. *Collector's Guide to American Art Pottery*. New York: Crown Publishers, 1974. 271 pp., illus.

Kovel, Ralph M., and Terry J. Kovel. *Dictionary of Marks: Pottery and Porcelain*. New York: Crown Publishers, 1953. 278 pp., illus.

Litchfield, Frederick. *Pottery and Porcelain: A Guide to Collectors*. 6th ed., rev. New York: M. Barrows, 1964. 356 pp., illus., bibliog.

Mankowitz, Wolf, and Reginald G. Haggar. *The Concise Encyclopedia of English Pottery and Porcelain*. New York: Praeger, 1968. 312 pp., illus., bibliog.

Ray, Marcia. *Collectible Ceramics: An Encyclopedia of Pottery and Porcelain for the American Collector*. New York: Crown Publishers, 1974. 256 pp., illus.

Sandon, Henry. *British Pottery and Porcelain for Pleasure and Investment*. New York: Arco Publishing Co., 1969. 175 pp., illus.

Schwartz, Marvin D. *Collectors Guide to Antique American Ceramics*. New York: Doubleday, 1969. 134 pp., illus.

Theus, Will H., *How to Detect and Collect Antique Porcelain and Pottery: A Practical Primer for the Beginning Collector*. New York: Alfred A. Knopf, 1974. 249 pp., illus.

Furniture

Bishop, Robert C. *Guide to American Antique Furniture*. New York: Galahad, 1975. 224 pp., illus., bibliog.

Comstock, Helen. *American Furniture, Seventeenth, Eighteenth, and Nineteenth Century Styles*. New York: Viking Press, 1962. 336 pp., illus., bibliog.

Downs, Joseph. *American Furniture: Queen Anne and Chippendale Periods in the Henry Francis du Pont Winterthur Museum.* New York: Bonanza Books, 1952. 400 pp., illus.

Fales, Dean A., Jr. *American Painted Furniture, 1660–1880.* New York: Dutton, 1972. 299 pp., illus., bibliog.

Grotz, George. *The New Antiques: Knowing and Buying Victorian Furniture.* New York: Doubleday, 1964. 224 pp., illus.

Hayward, Helena, ed. *World Furniture: An Illustrated History.* New York: McGraw-Hill, 1965. 320 pp., illus., bibliog.

Hinkley, F. Lewis. *A Directory of Antique Furniture: The Authentic Classification of European and American Designs for Professionals and Connoisseurs.* New York: Crown Publishers, 1953. 355 pp., illus.

Kirk, John T. *Early American Furniture: How to Recognize, Evaluate, Buy, and Care for the Most Beautiful Pieces—High-Style, Country, Primitive, and Rustic.* New York: Alfred A. Knopf, 1974. 208 pp., illus.

Kovel, Ralph M., and Terry J. Kovel. *American Country Furniture, 1780–1875.* New York: Crown Publishers, 1965. 248 pp., illus., bibliog.

Montgomery, Charles F. *American Furniture: The Federal Period in the Henry Francis du Pont Winterthur Museum.* New York: Bonanza Books, 1978. 497 pp., illus., bibliog.

Nutting, Wallace. *Furniture Treasury (Mostly of American Origin).* 7th printing. New York: Macmillan, 1968. 3 vols., illus.

Ormsbee, Thomas H. *Field Guide to American Victorian Furniture.* New York: Bonanza Books, 1964. 428 pp., illus.

Ormsbee, Thomas H. *Field Guide to Early American Furniture.* Boston: Little, Brown & Co., 1951. 464 pp., illus., bibliog.

Ramsey, L. G. G., and Helen Comstock, eds. *Antique Furniture: The Guide for Collectors, Investors and Dealers.* New York: Hawthorn Books, 1969. 362 pp., illus.

Sack, Albert. *Fine Points of Furniture: Early American.* New York: Crown Publishers, 1950. 303 pp., illus.

Schwartz, Marvin D. *Chairs, Tables, Sofas & Beds.* New York: Alfred A. Knopf, 1982. 480 pp., illus., bibliog.

Glass

Corning, N.Y., Museum of Glass. *Glass from the Corning Museum of Glass: A Guide to the Collections.* Rev. ed. Corning, N.Y.: Corning Glass Center, 1974. 105 pp., illus., bibliog.

Duncan, George S. *Bibliography of Glass.* Edited by Violet Dimbleby. Dobbs Ferry, N.Y.: Oceana Publications, 1960. 544 pp.

Gros-Galliner, Gabriella. *Glass: A Guide for Collectors.* New York: Stein & Day, 1970. 175 pp., illus., bibliog.

Lee, Ruth Webb. *Early American Pressed Glass: A Classification of Patterns Collectible in Sets Together with Individual Pieces for Table Decorations.* 36th ed. Wellesley Hills, Mass.: Lee Publications, 1960. 666 pp., illus.

Lee, Ruth Webb. *Handbook of Early American Pressed Glass Patterns.* Wellesley Hills, Mass.: Lee Publications, 1964. 216 pp., illus.

Lee, Ruth Webb. *Sandwich Glass: The History of the Boston and Sandwich Glass*

Company. 10th ed. Wellesley Hills, Mass.: Lee Publications, 1966. 590 pp., illus.

McKearin, George S., and Helen McKearin. *American Glass*. New York: Crown Publishers, 1966. 634 pp., illus., bibliog.

Munsey, Cecil. *The Illustrated Guide to Collecting Bottles*. New York: Hawthorn Books, 1970. 308 pp., illus., bibliog.

Pearson, J. Michael, and Dorothy T. Pearson. *American Cut Glass for the Discriminating Collector*. New York: Vantage Press, 1965. 204 pp., illus.

Peterson, Arthur Goodwin. *400 Trademarks on Glass*. Takoma Park, Md.: Washington College Press, 1967. 52 pp., illus.

Revi, Albert C. *Nineteenth Century Glass, Its Genesis and Development*. Rev. ed. New York: Thomas Nelson & Sons, 1967. 301 pp., illus.

Spillman, Jane Shadel. *Glass Tableware, Bowls, & Vases*. New York: Alfred A. Knopf, 1982. 480 pp., illus., bibliog.

Metal

Clayton, Michael. *The Collector's Dictionary of the Silver and Gold of Great Britain and North America*. New York: World Publishing Co., 1971. 352 pp., illus., bibliog.

Ebert, Katherine. *Collecting American Pewter*. New York: Charles Scribner's Sons, 1973. 163 pp., illus., bibliog.

Henderson, James. *Silver Collecting for Amateurs*. New York: Barnes and Noble, 1968. 144 pp., illus.

McClinton, Katharine Morrison. *Collecting American 19th Century Silver*. New York: Charles Scribner's Sons, 1968. 280 pp., illus., bibliog.

Montgomery, Charles F. *A History of American Pewter*. New York: Praeger, 1973. 246 pp., illus., bibliog.

Peal, Christopher A. *British Pewter and Britannia Metal: For Pleasure and Investment*. New York: International Publications Service, 1971. 200 pp., illus., bibliog.

Rainwater, Dorothy T., and H. Ivan Rainwater. *American Silverplate*. Nashville, Tenn.: T. Nelson, 1972. 480 pp., illus., bibliog.

Schwartz, Marvin D. *Collectors' Guide to Antique American Silver*. Garden City, N.Y.: Doubleday, 1975. 174 pp., illus., bibliog.

Taylor, Gerald. *Silver*. Baltimore, Md.: Penguin Books, 1963. 301 pp., illus., bibliog.

Wyler, Seymour B. *The Book of Old Silver: English, American, Foreign; With All Available Hallmarks, Including Sheffield Plate Marks*. New York: Crown Publishers, 1937. 447 pp., illus.

Specialized Collecting

Anderton, Johana Gast. *Twentieth Century Dolls: From Bisque to Vinyl*. North Kansas City, Mo.: Athena Publishing Co., 1974. 464 pp., illus.

Andrews, Ruth, ed. *How to Know American Folk Art*. New York: Dutton, 1977. 204 pp., illus.

Arbor, Marilyn, et al. *Tools and Trades of America's Past: The Mercer Collection*. Doyleston, Pa.: Bucks County Historical Society, 1981. 116 pp., illus.

Barlow, Ronald S. *The Antique Tool Collector's Guide to Value*. El Cajon, Ca.: Windmill Publications Co., 1985. 229 pp., illus.

Celehar, Jane H. *Kitchen and Kitchenware*. Lombard, Ill.: Wallace-Homestead, 1985. 208 pp., illus., bibliog.

Ebert, John, and Katherine Ebert. *Old American Prints for the Collector*. New York: Charles Scribner's Sons, 1974. 277 pp., illus., bibliog.

Levitt, Wendy. *Dolls*. New York: Alfred A. Knopf, 1983. 480 pp., illus.

Lipman, Jean, and Alice Winchester. *The Flowering of American Folk Art 1776–1876*. New York: Viking Press, 1974. 288 pp., illus., bibliog.

McClintock, Inez, and Marshall McClintock. *Toys in America*. Washington, D.C.: Public Affairs Press, 1961. 480 pp., illus., bibliog.

Thompson, Frances. *Antique Baskets and Basketry*. Lombard, Ill.: Wallace-Homestead, 1985. 96 pp., illus.

Weinstein, Robert A., and Larry Booth. *Collection, Use and Care of Historical Photographs*. Nashville, Tenn.: American Association for State and Local History, 1977. 222 pp., illus., bibliog.

Textiles and Costumes

Arnold, Janet. *A Handbook of Costume*. London: Macmillan, 1973. 336 pp., illus., bibliog.

Bishop, Robert C. *Quilts, Coverlets, Rugs & Samplers*. New York: Alfred A. Knopf. 480 pp., illus., bibliog.

Davenport, Millia. *The Book of Costume*. 3rd printing. New York: Crown Publishers, 1964. 2 vols., 958 pp., illus., bibliog.

Gans-Ruedin, E. *The Connoisseur's Guide to Oriental Carpets*. Rutland, Vt.: Charles E. Tuttle, 1971. 430 pp., illus., bibliog.

Head, R. E. *Lace & Embroidery Collector: A Guide to Collectors of Old Lace and Embroidery*. 1922. Reprint. Ann Arbor, Mich.: Gryphon Books, 1971. 252 pp., illus., bibliog.

Jacobsen, Charles W. *Check Points on How to Buy Oriental Rugs*. Rutland, Vt.: Charles E. Tuttle, 1969. 208 pp., illus.

Jacobsen, Charles W. *Oriental Rugs: A Complete Guide*. Rutland, Vt.: Charles E. Tuttle, 1973. 479 pp., illus., bibliog.

Khin, Yvonne M. *The Collector's Dictionary of Quilt Names*. Washington, D.C.: Acropolis Books Ltd., 1985. 489 pp., illus., bibliog.

Laver, James. *The Concise History of Costume and Fashion*. New York: Charles Scribner's Sons, 1974. 228 pp., illus., bibliog.

Stafford, Carleton, and Robert Bishop. *America's Quilts and Coverlets*. New York: Dutton, 1972. 313 pp., illus., bibliog.

INDEX

OCT 9 0

RODMAN PUBLIC LIBRARY
215 East Broadway
Alliance, OH   44601